W9-AQE-739

TWAYNE'S WORLD AUTHORS SERIES

A Survey of the World's Literature

Sylvia E. Bowman, Indiana University

GENERAL EDITOR

SPAIN

Gerald E. Wade, Vanderbilt University

EDITOR

Camilo José Cela

(*TWAS 67*)

TWAYNE'S WORLD AUTHORS SERIES (TWAS)

The purpose of TWAS is to survey the major writers —novelists, dramatists, historians, poets, philosophers, and critics—of the nations of the world. Among the national literatures covered are those of Australia, Canada, China, Eastern Europe, France, Germany, Greece, India, Italy, Japan, Latin America, New Zealand, Poland, Russia, Scandinavia, Spain, and the African nations, as well as Hebrew, Yiddish, and Latin Classical literatures. This survey is complemented by Twayne's United States Authors Series and English Authors Series

The intent of each volume in these series is to present a critical-analytical study of the works of the writer; to include biographical and historical material that may be necessary for understanding, appreciation, and critical appraisal of the writer; and to present all material in clear, concise English—but not to vitiate the scholarly content of the work by doing so.

Camilo José Cela

By D. W. McPHEETERS

Newcomb College
Tulane University

Twayne Publishers, Inc.   ::   New York

Copyright © 1969 by Twayne Publishers, Inc.

All Rights Reserved

Library of Congress Catalog Card Number: 74-75876

CAMILO JOSÉ CELA

863.64
M172

12-8-69 - direct - $4.95

Preface

THIS book is intended to present to a general public the life and works of Spain's leading novelist since the Civil War of 1936-1939. Because there exist contradictory ideas of Spanish life and culture, an attempt has been made, where feasible, to qualify any broad statements with sufficient nuances to allow for diverse attitudes. Cela himself has observed that organizational support at home and abroad facilitates the entry of foreign novelists into the international arena, but for the Spanish writer, there is no such backing. Quite the contrary. This situation, of course, has not been helped by periods, including the most recent, when Spain's historical role isolated her from the mainstream of Western intellectual and political thought. An explanation of the peculiarities of the national mentality is not to be sought solely in the romantic, exotic civilization of the past, however imposing the monuments to this culture. Spain clings to her traditional, albeit essentially European, institutions which possess as well their own indigenous quality. Such a difference makes the country intriguing, but it complicates the efforts of a Spanish writer to achieve international standing.

Camilo José Cela appeared dramatically on the literary scene in 1942 with *La familia de Pascual Duarte* (*The Family of Pascual Duarte*), which not only caused a sensation, but, more important, secured a wide foreign acceptance. It has the virtues and defects of a first novel. Even greater acclaim for *La colmena* (*The Hive*), 1951—a work of maturity and originality without the earlier shortcomings—assured his place at mid-century as one of Europe's outstanding novelists. In view of Spain's internal and

73999

international situation, his accomplishment is all the more remarkable, indicating that these books were sufficiently timely to receive immediate attention.

My study of Cela offers no specific critical approach or thesis; it seeks to review the author's literary output—with the exception of his poetry that is considered here as a reflection of a lyric vein to be found in almost all his writings. A reading and re-reading of the texts give evidence of recurring elements and themes which, when noteworthy, are pointed out. A balanced view of the various facets of Cela's personality based on his works, published biographical material, and personal conversations reveals that he is a much more complex individual than has been generally believed. An early aggressive, but generous behavior led to a certain public image—the result of his endeavor to develop a literary style and establish an independence of spirit in the face of postwar apathy and the strictures of censorship. Yet he is on occasion introversive—not, one hastens to add, in the highly pejorative sense that he sometimes uses the term—and he may even display timidity. An intense sensitivity expresses itself in compassion for children and social outcasts, in affection for animals and even wild flowers, and this tenderness is offset by wit, irony, and humor—at times, earthy, at times grotesque. His courtesy and refined manners surprise more than one interviewer who obviously expect his conduct to conform to popular anecdote or to that of the characters of his novels. He has a strong sense of filial and fraternal ties and does not hide his paternal sentiments. His undeniable bluntness of speech reflects sincerity and the idiosyncrasies of an exceptional temperament.

After a review of his novels, short stories, sketches, and travel books, it is apparent that more space could be devoted to some, probably all, but it is hoped that, even though they have had brief treatment, their essential characteristics have not been distorted. Any adverse opinions are minor in an over-all survey of his total production and serve to point up, by contrast, the stature the novelist achieves in his best creations. The development of Cela's literary craftsmanship in three phases is emphasized.

The first is that of the violence, and even melodrama, of the earliest "tremendista" and possibly existentialist tendencies—a period in which he also wrote excellent short stories. The second, marking the peak of his creativity, comes with *La colmena*. After he left the milieu of Madrid literati to live with small-town people in Cebreros and to hike through the Alcarria, his powers of observation became acute: with few words— no more than a bit of dialogue, a grimace, a gesture—he captured the main traits of an individual. Increasing later financial prosperity may come to mean that he wrote most effectively and incisively in the struggling, hungry years when he was trying to earn a living from literature.

In a third phase, especially observable in *La Catira* (*The Blonde*), 1955, and continuing to the present, his style takes on a baroque richness ranging from linguistic virtuosity to crudity, concealing less originality and at the same time indirectly expressing personal feelings and beliefs. His writing is seldom dull, and he has the one fundamental talent: he is a good storyteller.

It is my hope that this account will serve as a guide to a many-sided author and that it will permit the assimilation of more particularized criticism. Since the best commentaries available note the importance of composition to Cela—a factor that others either have not understood or have chosen to ignore—I emphasize the structure of his books.

Most of the translations, except for those from *The Hive,* are mine. Either certain material in English was not at hand, or else I felt that my version rendered better the implications of the passages in question. No unfavorable criticism of the excellent translations into English which have appeared in the last few years is implied. I wish to thank Farrar, Straus, and Giroux, Inc. for permission to quote from *The Hive,* translated by J. M. Cohen, in consultation with Arturo Barea, copyright 1953. All gratitude is due to my wife whose aid and encouragement have far exceeded mere competence as a typist.

D. W. McPheeters

Newcomb College, Tulane University

CAMILO JOSÉ CELA
by

D. W. McPHEETERS

This study presents a critical appraisal and traces the literary development of one of Spain's best-known living authors. Camilo José Cela (b. 1916), who gained an international reputation with *La familia de Pascual Duarte* (1942) and *La colmena* (1951). In spite of censorship and the indifference of both writers and the general public after the Civil War (1936-1939), *Pascual Duarte* helped to revive the Spanish novel and to restore to it something of its traditional prestige. Cela is the author of numerous other significant works displaying original themes and structure which have influenced writers throughout the Hispanic world. A member of the Real Academia Española de la Lengua and publisher of the successful literary monthly *Papeles de Son Armadans,* as well as sponsor of various literary activities in Palma, Majorca, and elsewhere, Cela continues to play a leading role in literary affairs. His artistic and intellectual integrity, renewed interest in common people as a source of inspiration, varied and polished style, and narrative skill recommend him to the reader. Cela has visited the United States on two occasions—in 1964 and 1966—the first time for a period of six months to give a series of lectures and to receive the Doctor of Letters degree, *honoris causa,* from Syracuse University.

Contents

Chronology

1916 May 11: Born at Iria-Flavia, province of La Coruña, Spain.
1919 First trip to England.
1921 Primary school in Vigo, administered by the nuns of St. Joseph de Cluny.
1923 Enters elementary school of the Jesuits in Vigo.
1925 Family settles permanently in Madrid.
1933 Graduates from secondary school.
1934 Enters tuberculosis sanitarium for first time. Studies medicine at Central University of Madrid for one year, 1934-1935. Friendship with and encouragement from Pedro Salinas.
1935 Published first poems in *El Argentino*, a daily of La Plata, Argentina.
1936 Volume of poetry, *Pisando la dudosa luz del día*, not published until 1945.
1937 Begins service in the Nationalist Army.
1938 Wounded while on army duty.
1939 Discharged from army with rank of corporal. Returns to Madrid. Begins study of law.
1940 First articles published in Spain. Begins writing *La familia de Pascual Duarte*.

1941	First short stories, including "Marcelo Brito" in *Medina*. Enters tuberculosis sanitarium for second time.
1942	First edition of *La familia de Pascual Duarte* in Burgos. Abandons law studies.
1943	Second edition of *La familia de Pascual Duarte* confiscated by the censor. *Pabellón de reposo*.
1944	March 12: Marries María del Rosario Conde Picavea. *Nuevas andanzas y desventuras de Lazarillo de Tormes*.
1945	*Esas nubes que pasan. Mesa revuelta.*
1946	January 17: Son Camilo José is born. Cela goes on walking tour in the summer through the Alcarria.
1947	*El bonito crimen del carabinero y otras invenciones*, a collection of short stories.
1948	*Viaje a la Alcarria.*
1949	*El gallego y su cuadrilla, y otros apuntes carpetovetónicos.*
1951	*La colmena* printed in Argentina; publication prohibited in Spain.
1952	Trip to Argentina and Chile. *Del Miño al Bidasoa, notas de un vagabundaje*.
1953	*Baraja de invenciones. Mrs. Caldwell habla con su hijo.* Second trip to South America.
1954	Beginning of residence in Palma, Majorca. Lecture trip to England.
1955	*La Catira.* Third trip to South America.
1956	Begins publishing literary monthly, *Papeles de Son Armadans. Judíos, moros y cristianos. El molino de viento y otras novelas cortas.*
1957	May 26: Reception into Royal Spanish Academy. *Cajón de sastre. La rueda de los ocios. Historias de España: Los ciegos, Los tontos.*
1958	Two trips to France. Friendship with Pablo Picasso.
1959	Another trip to France. *Primer viaje andaluz. La cucaña, memorias de Camilo José Cela.*
1960	*Los viejos amigos*, first series. *Cuatro figuras del '98, Unamuno, Valle-Inclán, Baroja, Azorín.*
1961	*Los viejos amigos*, second series.
1962	*Tobogán de hambrientos. Gavilla de fábulas sin amor,*

illustrated by Picasso, allowed by the censorship, but no press commentary permitted. *Obra completa*, I.

1963 *El solitario. Toreo de salón. Once cuentos de fútbol. Las compañías convenientes. Garito de hospicianos.*

1964 Lecture tour in the United States and honorary doctoral degree from Syracuse University. *Izas, rabizas y colipoterras. Obra completa*, II.

1965 Short trip to Havana. *Viaje al Pirineo de Lérida. Páginas de geografía errabunda. El ciudadano Iscariote Reclús. Nuevas escenas matritenses*, series 1-2. *Obra completa*, III, IV.

1966 *Nuevas escenas matritenses*, series 3-7. *Madrid. Obra completa*, V. Second trip to the United States.

1967 *Viaje a U. S. A.*

1968 October 20: Speech of welcome on the occasion of the reception of Antonio Rodríguez-Moñino into the Spanish Academy. *Obra completa*, VI. *Diccionario secreto*, I.

CHAPTER 1

The Story of a Writer

A T first glance Cela seems to have spoken rather freely about his life, particularly his childhood and youth, in memoirs, prologues to editions of his works, various short pieces in *Papeles de Son Armadans,* the periodical he publishes, and in interviews.[1] On reviewing these comments, however, one realizes that they tell what the novelist is willing to reveal of his own life up to a certain point and no more. Of course, his accounts of travels throughout Spain, his many sketches of popular types, and his short stories are sprinkled with numerous remarks which reveal a personal outlook. For the special number of *Revista Hispánica Moderna,* New York, 1962, dedicated to Cela, he supplied an autobiographical sketch based largely on material brought together from earlier publications.

I *In Search of a Career*

Cela was born May 11, 1916, in the Galician town of Iria-Flavia, one of the most beautiful place names anywhere, according to him, and one which still preserves intact its old Roman form. His mother, Camila Enmanuela Trulock y Bertorini, though Galician, was of English nationality until her marriage; her mother, of English and Italian origin, had married John Trulock, who, like great-grandfather Bertorini, was manager of The West Galician Railway. Even after forty-three years in Spain Trulock still spoke an Anglicized Spanish. The Trulocks were of Cornish stock. Those who like to speculate on atavistic traits might wonder what sort of character would result from a fusion of two Celtic strains—the Welsh and Galician. The one person known to me who most resembles Cela in physical type and bluntness of expression is a Chicagoan of Welsh parentage.

Cela's father, Camilo Cela y Fernández, was a customs official; his was a profession which necessitated, in the early years of the author's life, frequent moves by the family so that, except for chance, the son might have been born in Andalusia and have had quite a different personality. This is an amusing observation that is difficult to take seriously. The father's family was deeply rooted in Galicia. On occasion in typical Galician fashion the novelist, displaying an obvious, nostalgic love for the region, traces the numerous relatives—some far removed—scattered about the province. His reserved, strong-willed father was a difficult man for him to know; each thought the other stupid until both came to realize that such was not the case at all. The father may naturally have felt that literature was hardly a suitable career for his eldest son, although he himself had had some experience as a writer. The trait that most impressed the boy was his father's sincere, absolute disdain for death.

One of seven living children, Cela was baptized Camilo José Manuel Juan Ramón Francisco Santiago. At one time he playfully added the Jewish names Zacarías, Abraham, and David as a protest against the Nazis and their Aryan nonsense; for variety, he would substitute Leví for David. This bit of whimsy produced curious results at the time of his reception into the Spanish Academy when *Amanecer,* a Jewish newspaper in Buenos Aires, dedicated a special feature to him on March 23, 1957, with the statement that in Monarchist, Ultramontane, Falangist Spain the writer had never concealed his Jewish origin.

Cela was always a child of delicate health, and a serious fall endangered his life. He was also an indifferent student and has unpleasant memories of his studies at several secondary schools administered by religious orders, but he did manage to graduate from the Instituto de San Isidro of the Marist fathers in Madrid. He must have been a very observant youngster because years later, in his memoirs, he will describe charmingly, with almost total recall, the first years in Galicia with reminiscences of local places and people, as well as numerous trips, including a visit to an aunt in England. At an early age he developed an interest in poetry and as a young versifier wrote rather unoriginal compositions; yet the lyric part of his literary output, while not large, is significant and, later, quite creditable. His poetic sensitivity is a valuable aspect of his books of vagabondage, for example, and serves to temper more truculent passages.

At the age of eighteen came Cela's first bout with tuberculosis,[2] and in 1941 he was again forced to enter a sanitarium. No doubt these experiences heightened a tendency to introspection; one novel, *Pabellón de reposo* (*The Sanitarium*), recounts life in just such an institution. Paradoxically, more than anything else attempts to combat these periods of ill health in all probability determined his future character and career. In overcoming physical weakness, and partly as a result of it, Cela was to acquire a cultural background and to develop a moral strength and true literary vocation.

His memoirs speak of an adolescent fascination with the Nietzschean philosophy of the will: "Let the weakling fall by the wayside; he should not hinder the march of others. The will is the tool of success and more important than intelligence. One should not make a single false step, a single step which does not lead to the proposed goal,"[3] and so on. The writings of Ortega restored his morale and reoriented a young man confused by Nietzsche and demoralized by church-run schools.

It was during the long periods of convalescence after first being hospitalized with tuberculosis that the boy read through the entire seventy-volume collection of Spanish classical authors (*Biblioteca de Autores Españoles*), using the seventy-first, or index tome, to keep track of his readings. These are thick, aesthetically unattractive works, generally with two columns to a page, but they contain nearly all the older Spanish writers. Cela tells us that he did not skip around and, when his mind wandered, would go back and reread that page. Each fat tome was a triumph. Thus, the future novelist acquired a grounding in the literary traditions of Spain that many a professional

Hispanist might envy. Erudition was not the goal of this reading; possibly he himself only vaguely sensed where this preparation might lead. His favorites were such humane writers as
Lope de Vega, Cervantes, Santa Teresa, Quevedo, San Juan
de la Cruz, Fray Luis de León, the Archpriest of Hita, Santillana,
Jorge Manrique, and Jovellanos; he did not care for the more
intellectual Calderón, Fray Luis de Granada, Tirso, and
Moratín.

Significantly, he read Dostoevski and reread the first (1554)
and most popular of the picaresque novels, *Lazarillo de Tormes*.
According to Eugenio d'Ors, the writer who is not rooted in
his native tradition is of necessity a plagiarist;[4] this is an
especially pertinent observation when applied to Spanish writers
whose imitations of foreign works are often quite bad. It is
not surprising, then, that the third novel to come from Cela's
pen was a revival of the adventures of Lazarillo, *Nuevas andanzas y desventuras de Lazarillo de Tormes (New Wanderings
and Misfortunes of Lazarillo de Tormes)*, 1944.

As a young man Cela was evidently something of an *esprit-
fort* who "confused moderation with cowardice" and wrote a
new code of civil law, "hard and liberal at the same time."
Accordingly, he reflected certain ideological currents popular
among many young people in Spain which led to an involvement with the National Socialist movement and the founding of
the Falange by the charismatic José Antonio Primo de Rivera,
whose magnetism was admitted even by his Marxist enemies.
This movement hoped to revive Spanish traditional values;
ironically, since Spanish tradition had much that was incompatible with modern fascism, it was inevitable that the deep-
rooted religious spirit of the people would mitigate at least
some of Nazism's more obnoxious features. Cela is seldom a
tendentious writer, either because he has a perspective grounded
in Spanish classical literature, or because he possesses a high
degree of personal integrity, or perhaps because of both. But
he has always had the courage to express himself frankly, even
forthrightly, a penchant which has led to problems with an
overly squeamish censorship.

The young poet, for poetry remained his literary pastime,
continued composing verse and indulging in a number of casual

friendships with the fair sex. At age eighteen, after trips to
France and England, he began the study of medicine during
the academic year 1934-1935. At the same time he also presented himself to the distinguished poet-teacher Pedro Salinas
at the Junta de Ampliación de Estudios, and his attendance at
the latter's literature classes at the University of Madrid decided him on his future career.

His first poems appeared in 1935 in the Argentine daily, *El
Argentino* of La Plata, together with a verbal self-portrait and
a sketch by Luis Enrique Délano, fellow student at the Faculty
of Philosophy and Letters of the University. Délano was a
secretary of the Chilean consulate when Gabriela Mistral, future
Nobel Prize winner, and Pablo Neruda were consuls. Cela
still admits with some pride the influence of Neruda on his
book of poetry, *Pisando la dudosa luz del día (Treading the Uncertain Light of Day)*, 1936, a title derived from a line in *La
fábula de Polifemo y Galatea (The Fable of Polyphemus and
Galatea)*, by the great baroque poet Góngora. The revival of
interest in Góngora's linguistically obscure work on the part
of various poets and critics was an important new trend in
Spanish poetry of the late twenties and early thirties. Meanwhile Isaías Cabezón offered to paint Cela's portrait for a fee
of twenty thousand pesetas, a ludicrously large sum for the
period and particularly for the young poet whose mother gave
him an allowance of ten pesetas every Sunday and occasionally
six or eight more during the week. This impecuniousness was
to last for several years more, even after the publication of
Pascual Duarte.

With the uprising in Morocco of July 17, 1936, the Spanish
Civil War began. Cela was declared unfit for military service
because of his tubercular condition. Evacuated through Valencia
on the British relief ship "Maine," he was accepted for duty
by the Nationalist forces after his health improved. In 1938 he
suffered injuries from shrapnel and a bullet wound in the
thigh. Some of his poetry of these war years, such as "Himno a
la muerte" ("Hymn to Death"), 1938, was also published in
Argentina. In his prologue to the first book of memoirs (1959),
he states that within fifteen or twenty years he will write his

own novel of the Spanish Civil War. He has proposed *La hoguera (The Pyre)*, as the subtitle for a projected Book IV of his reminiscences. In recent correspondence he has informed me that he is at work on a narrative of the conflict.

In 1939 Cela was discharged from the army with the rank of corporal, and he immediately began the study of law, only to abandon it after three years and some courses of the fourth and fifth years. His commentary on a series of family photographs of the novelist Emilia Pardo Bazán appeared in 1940, the first composition to be printed in Spain (I, 555). In that same year he began writing the novel that was to gain him international recognition, *La familia de Pascual Duarte*, composed in the kitchen of the Textile Syndicate in Madrid where he worked as clerk. He read selections as soon as he wrote them to friends at the Café Gijón, a meeting place for writers. The date is of some importance because there are critics who find that Cela imitated *The Stranger* (1942) of Albert Camus. In one edition of his novel Cela stated erroneously that he had read these selections in 1941, but in the *Obra completa (Complete Works)*, I, 553, he has since corrected that date. The whole question, actually, is rather trivial since *Pascual Duarte* bears only a casual resemblance to the French novel. For the present, suffice it to say, Cela expressed his unqualified admiration for Camus one hot July afternoon in 1964 as he drove me back to my modest pension in the quiet little resort of Santa Ponsa, far around the bay of Palma.

At the end of 1941 he fell seriously ill again, deathly so, as he thought then, but recollection provokes the wry remark, "Dying, which seems at times so easy, is, on other occasions, more difficult than one might imagine" (I, 551). On the Day of the Three Kings, 1942, he called for his notebooks and wrote the final pages of *Pascual Duarte*. Several publishers turned down the manuscript either because they preferred better-known authors or because they feared unfavorable reaction from government censorship. Having read the work on a train trip, the discerning scholar and critic, José María de Cossío, was impressed with it, and finally Aldecoa of Burgos published it— on a press in the garage of a bus line, Continental-Auto— December 28, 1942.

The second edition of *Pascual Duarte* was printed in November of the following year. Pío Baroja, Spain's leading novelist for forty years, refused to write the prologue, declaring that it was all right for a young man like Cela to go to prison if he wished, but he could do so alone (I, 560). No prison sentence materialized, but the second edition was confiscated, although by then nearly all the copies had been sold. Not even the author himself was able to find a copy of the first edition to give to the noted painter Ignacio de Zuloaga for his wife in Paris. Almost immediately the novel attracted attention in England and, on a program of the BBC, was compared with *Uncle Tom's Cabin*, undoubtedly because this book was enjoying a momentary revival. Translations into almost all European languages soon followed.

During these same years Cela was also publishing some of his best short stories which today are included in many anthologies. Since he had been quite ill while writing his first novel, in 1942 he found himself in the tuberculosis sanitarium of Dr. Valdés Lambea for a long period of recuperation. Toward the end of February, 1943, he began writing *Pabellón de reposo*, in which are presented the tragic minutiae of the lives of tubercular patients awaiting death.

II *The Successful Author*

Already in 1943, if not somewhat earlier, Cela had begun accumulating the details he was to fit together in *La colmena* (1951), a story having to do with three days in the lives of numerous persons in Madrid during the winter of 1943, a period of hardship, the aftermath of the Civil War. On March 12, 1944, he married María del Rosario Conde Picavea, "Charo," who had been his fiancée for some time. This attractive woman has helped her husband immeasurably; she is, among other things, the "secretary" to whom he often turns at a moment's notice to locate whatever manuscript or book he may need. And it was in this same year that his version of the famous picaresque novel, *Lazarillo de Tormes*, was published. Up to this point critics had considered him primarily a writer concerned with rural and small-town themes. This taste for the open-ended picaresque genre is a facet of his literary personality, later to be transmuted into the books of vagabondage and brief sketches of people and places such as those assembled in *Mesa revuelta (The Artist's Table)*, 1945. Then appeared the first collection of short stories, *Esas nubes que pasan (The Passing Clouds)*, twelve tales that had first been printed in periodicals. He literally tore them out of the magazines and sent them to a publisher anxious to print something by the new author now the center of so much attention. Cela himself says that at a time when he was doing nothing, he did not seem to have time to write anything (II, 31).

Anyone who has heard Cela proudly making plans for the education and future career of Camilo José, his son, will realize the importance to him of the birth of his only child on January 17, 1946. Later, from June 6-15 of that year, he undertook a walking tour of the Alcarria, a little-known region a short distance northeast of Madrid. His stays in the sanitarium must have done him good, he once remarked, because he was able to make the long daily hikes without falling by the wayside. It is of course quite possible that such walks were the best "medicine" available for his chronic tubercular condition.

Between December 25 and 31 of 1947 Cela wrote up the notes made during the trip to the Alcarria and the book came out the following year as *Viaje a la Alcarria (Journey to the Alcarria)*. In 1947 was published *El bonito crimen del carabinero y otras invenciones (The Neat Crime of the Carabiniere and Other Tales)*, a collection of short stories; one chapter—first printed in the newspaper *Arriba*, April 25, 1946—will later be included in revised form in his novel *La colmena*, on which he was now working steadily. He spent part of the summers of 1947, 1948, 1949, and 1950 in the little town of Cebreros in the hot, lower region of the province of Ávila, at some distance from the mountains and high Castilian mesa. During the second summer he wrote one of the numerous drafts of *La colmena*— there were five in all—using a marble-topped table in the cramped, tiny kitchen on the second floor of a house in El Azoguejo, the Little Market, as its quaint Moorish name indicates. The proprietor of the Madrid, one of the town's four cafés, lent Cela a table.

It was while staying in Cebreros that he also began writing the "apuntes carpetovetónicos" or little surprised chronicles of the minuscule happenings of the dry sections of Spain. These resemble etchings; in fact, the author says that they must be associated with scenes from the arid lands of the peninsula. Most of these sketches appeared in dailies of the period, to be collected for the first time in the *Complete Works* (III, 1965); nevertheless, a few are to be found in *El gallego y su cuadrilla y otros apuntes carpetovetónicos (The Galician and his Troupe and Other Carpeto-Vettonian Notes)*, first printed in a rather modest volume in Toledo, 1949, but which did not reach bookstores until 1951.

The sojourns in Cebreros were fundamental for Cela's literary development. Here he lost the aloofness of the young middle-class gentleman and found in this humble, hungry environment the two poles, one human, one literary, which were basic for his future writings; here, too, he learned that one who perseveres wins out and that literature, like pottery, has to be nourished by the popular vitality. Cela comes to identify with the people as no other Spanish writers, even those of the Generation of 1898, had ever done, except, perhaps, Galdós in the nineteenth century. Attempting to make a living solely from creative writing, a difficult undertaking in Spain, he was often so short of money that he had to borrow the twenty-five or fifty pesetas—less than fifty cents or a dollar—for a simple meal and the bus trip to Madrid. During the months of July and August, 1948, he was commissioned by the Madrid daily, *Pueblo,* to make a second tour, this time by car, of the provinces to report on the summer hostels for vacationing workers. The first book relating these excursions, *Del Miño al Bidasoa (From the Miño to the Bidasoa),* was published in 1952.

Anecdotes illustrating his precarious financial position during this interim abound. He continued to write short stories for periodicals. One was dictated November 23, 1949, when he was suffering from a high fever and had not a cent in his apartment in Ríos Rosas, Madrid, where he still resides when in the Spanish capital. On looking back on the economic crises of these years, the author is stupefied.

In 1951 there was published in Argentina the second of his more important novels, *La colmena,* on which he had labored from 1945 to 1950. This work is a patiently constructed mosaic —Cela himself prefers to compare it to a watch—an implication that no piece of it can be omitted. It represents the culmination of the lapidary technique developed by Cela in Cebreros and applied to the urban setting of Madrid. He was at the peak of his creativity. A feeling of euphoria, therefore, may have induced him to claim that he was Spain's most important novelist since the Generation of 1898 (II, 543) and that in the writing of novels no method other than his was satisfactory; if he believed differently, he would seek another métier. As one can imagine, his remarks provoked unfavorable critical reaction. Sometimes of course he writes tongue-in-cheek, and yet one detects elements of truth in his statements. The Spanish novel, already in decline prior to the Civil War, had virtually ceased to exist as a worthy genre; almost single-handedly Cela had given it new life and international significance. His assertion as to technique is more debatable, but it had an impact; only a few years ago a fairly competent novelist remarked to me rather wistfully that, after the vogue of *La colmena,* the novel of the single protagonist was due for a revival.

The following year saw Cela on his first journey to South America; his Argentinian and Chilean publishers desired his presence in connection with editions of his works. Typical is his affirmation that he set out with little more than three dollars in his pockets. His most memorable experience was a meeting with the Italian writer, Curzio Malaparte, on the plane from Buenos Aires to Santiago. The two later stayed at the same hotel and almost became victims of an automobile accident in the mountains; fortunately the vehicle turned over in some bushes rather than on the cliff side of the road. The resultant publicity in Spain was considerable.

In the autumn of 1952 Cela put the final touches to *Mrs. Caldwell habla con su hijo (Mrs. Caldwell Talks with Her Son),* on which he had been working sporadically since 1947.

While on a fishing trip in the Sierra de Gredos in July, he prepared a meaningful prologue for the book. An illusion of continuity with earlier writings is achieved in his brief notice to the reader when he declares that he first met the eccentric Mrs. Caldwell during his tour of the Alcarria, the encounter taking place in the death chamber of the Princess of Eboli in the Palace of Pastrana. Mrs. Caldwell had been busily engaged in removing tiles from the bedroom of this sixteenth-century princess.

This novel was published in 1953, and the same year Cela made his second trip to South America, visiting this time Colombia, Ecuador, and Venezuela. The experiences of the two journeys have been combined in *La rueda de los ocios (The Wheel of Idle Moments)*, 1957, where the reader receives the erroneous impression that he made only one South American tour. While in Venezuela, Cela received an invitation from the Galician Center of Caracas to lecture on the theme "Homesickness in Galician Literature." He was also named Honorary Guest of the government and was commissioned to write a novel about Venezuela. This he completed under the title *La Catira* the year after he took up residence in Palma. It is here that the author still resides. His first residence was at José Villalonga, 87, near the Castle of Bellver with its beautiful view of the Bay of Palma, and in the summer of 1964 he moved to his new home at La Bonanova overlooking Illetas. Life in Majorca has been gratifying for Cela, where he has such friends and neighbors as Joan Miró, the poet Robert Graves, and Anthony Kerrigan, who is also the authorized English translator of his works.

La Catira was published in 1955, to be followed in 1956 by the third book of vagabondage, *Judíos, moros y cristianos (Jews, Moors, and Christians)*. It was also in 1956 that Cela began editing his literary journal *Papeles de Son Armadans*, a completely independent review, which has generally maintained high standards, with contributions from Spain's leading writers, timely criticism of foreign authors, and special numbers dedicated to such leading artists as Picasso, Joan Miró, and Gaudí. The rumor persists that Cela was subsidized by the rather unsavory industrialist Juan March of Barcelona, an allegation he firmly denies. Personal conversations with him in 1960 elicited the information that the journal has been financially quite successful, an assertion substantiated by the fact that even small college libraries in the United States usually subscribe.

Characteristically, Number VIII of *Papeles* (November, 1956) contains a moving tribute on the death October 30, 1956, of his early mentor, Pío Baroja, and his praise of the poet Juan Ramón Jiménez, who had just received the Nobel Prize. Two years after the death of Zenobia, the poet's wife, Cela published his earlier correspondence with her in which he revealed his long-cherished dream of seeing the two return to take up residence on Spanish soil.

Cela encountered the grieving Ernest Hemingway at Baroja's funeral and asked that he serve with him as pallbearer, but was refused with the words, "It is too great an honor for me. His friends . . . his old friends. . . ." And Cela replied, "As you wish" (*PSA, ibid.*, 131). He recalls Hemingway's words to Baroja shortly before the old novelist's death, the same words that appeared in *Time*, October 29, 1956:

Allow me to pay this small tribute to you who taught so much to those of us who wanted to be writers when we were young. I deplore the fact that you have not yet received a Nobel Prize, especially when it was given to so many who deserved it less, like me, who am only an adventurer.

Cela had been with Hemingway earlier, in February, at the Escorial, and in *Papeles*, Number IX, he dedicated a selection to him ". . . who presented me with *Death in the Afternoon* and a bottle of good wine." The empty container is now part of the collection which serves to remind him of various bottles shared with friends. On the occasion of Hemingway's death in 1961, Cela paid him a sincere tribute in Number LXIV of *Papeles*.

III *The Academy*

With 1957 came membership in the Royal Spanish Academy as its youngest member. Cela's speech of acceptance was entitled "La obra literaria de Solana" ("The Literary Work of Solana"), in which he discloses a great admiration for the popular themes and types portrayed by Solana in both his paintings and writings. The prominent critic and writer Dr. Gregorio Marañón, an old friend, read the speech of welcome. Solana had been asked to illustrate an edition of *La familia de Pascual Duarte* but had had to refuse because of failing eyesight, and Marañón had written the prologue for the edition of 1946, the first to be authorized in Spain after the book was banned in 1943. Its publication had been reconsidered because the Argentine edition of 1945 was circulating clandestinely; the censorship still objected to Marañón's prologue, but it was printed separately in *Insula*, 1946. Cela's independence of mind and artistic integrity are balanced by the attitude of members of his Rightist family, who did not consider him a successful writer until the Catholic daily *ABC* published his photograph reading his paper to the Academy with a minister, bishop, general, and the president Don Ramón Menéndez Pidal in the background.

With official recognition from the Academy and ever wider diffusion of his works and reputation, Cela has become something of a dean of Spanish novelists. Besides periodic trips to the mainland for business purposes or meetings of the Academy and longer excursions abroad, he has occasion frequently to play host to prominent visitors to Majorca. Among others, during the year 1958, there came the well-known Professor Ángel del Río of Columbia University, the poet Gerardo Diego, the gypsy dancer La Chunga, and, of course, Américo Castro, whom Cela had met in 1957 and who from time to time returns to the island for the summer. In May, 1959, Ramón Menéndez Pidal arrived in Palma to give a lecture, and during the week of May 18-25 Cela sponsored the Poetic Conversations, an informal get-together of poets, writers, and scholars, to discuss topics of mutual interest. Those attending included Alastair Read, Yves Bonnefoy, Vicente Aleixandre, Carles Riba, Dámaso Alonso, Anthony Kerrigan, Gerardo Diego, and Dionisio Ridruejo. Cela was also instrumental in having constructed the Poets' Club, where the committee of the Prix Formentor meets

on occasion. He is particularly proud of a photograph which
shows him with Adlai Stevenson, who also had read *La colmena,*
on the occasion of the bullfights held at Inca in July of that
year.

In 1960 and 1961 Cela published the two series of *Los
viejos amigos (The Old Friends),* short sketches in which he
again presents characters portrayed in earlier writings. They
have the independent existence of living persons—some at least
were—and this renewed contact gives immediacy to the narrative. He sets his people in motion and they carry on independently, or, lacking vitality, they die of boredom. Upon occasion correspondents write to comment about the death or
later situation of various personages, letters which he reports
in *Papeles.*

In the winter of 1960 the author made a long trip through
Southern France, lecturing at several French universities, and
resumed his acquaintance with Pablo Picasso, whom he had
interviewed in 1958 at his villa, La Californie, in connection
with the special number of *Papeles* dedicated to him, and with
whom he arranged for illustrations to accompany *Gavilla de
fábulas sin amor (A Bundle of Loveless Fables),* 1962, also
brought out by *Papeles.* The publication of this beautifully illustrated book of short texts and others such as *El solitario (The
Solitary One),* 1963, marks a new phase of Cela's literary production. Again, there are comments, with photographs, of a
pitiless but, at times, humorous realism, as in *Toreo de salón
(Drawing Room Bullfighting),* 1963, and *Izas, rabizas y colipoterras (Bawds, Harlots, and Hustlers),* 1964, Barcelona prostitutes. In 1965 and 1966 Cela published seven series of *Nuevas
escenas matritenses (New Scenes of Madrid),* in which each
text is accompanied by photographs of typical scenes of the
capital city. The *Once cuentos de fútbol (Eleven Football
Stories),* display colored pictures by eight-year-old Pepe. The
large originals now decorate a wall in Cela's new home in
Palma.

Cela continued to bring out numerous other volumes, including the *Obra completa,* beginning in 1962. During the first
six months of 1964 he gave a series of lectures at various uni-

versities in the United States, and the tour culminated on June 7 with his being awarded the degree of Doctor of Letters, honoris causa, by Syracuse University. Such recognition left him a bit bemused (*PSA,* no. XCVI [1964], xxxv-xxxvi); in spite of his various stints of university study, he had never received a degree.

In February, 1965, Cela was in Havana to serve on the jury for the awarding of the literary prize of the Casa de las Américas. In an unusually muddled open letter to Castro, *Papeles,* Number CVI, he urges the propagation of the term "Hispanoamérica" instead of "Latinoamérica" so commonly used by Yankee imperialists, since Spanish is the language of resistance of all Puerto Ricans who do not want to be a part of North American culture. He evidently chose to ignore the fact that Brazilians do not particularly care for the expression "Hispanoamérica," although it is often used in the United States, and that whenever a majority in Puerto Rico so votes, the island can become completely independent.

Cela is also associated with Ediciones Alfaguara which prints his works and those of other contemporary writers. He returned briefly to New York in March of 1966 for the International Writers' Conference at Long Island University, and in the summer of the same year lent his good offices as keynoter (*pregonero*) to the first Salon of the Bull to be celebrated in Soria from June to September, including the inauguration of a bullfighting museum.

During the past two years Cela's increasing status as dean of Spanish novelists becomes more evident. On December 14, 1967, a luncheon commemorating the twenty-fifth anniversary of the publication of *La familia de Pascual Duarte* was attended by many leading writers and academicians. A special issue of *Papeles,* Number CXLII, 1968, with pertinent observations by Gonzalo Sobejano and excellent illustrated bibliography by Huarte Morton also marks this event. On May 6, 1967, Cela spoke the words of welcome at a luncheon in honor of Severo Ochoa, co-winner of the Nobel Prize for medicine in 1959. One of the main events for Cela in 1968 was his reply to the reception speech of his old friend Antonio Rodríguez-Moñino when

he was received into the Spanish Academy; this occasion was
particularly gratifying to the many hispanists and admirers of
the distinguished scholar and bibliographer throughout the
world who have frequently attended his "tertulia" at the Café
León, the "tertulia" described in considerable detail in James
Michener's *Iberia* (361-63).

CHAPTER 2

A New Novelist of International Stature

WE have noted something of the circumstances surrounding the publication of *La familia de Pascual Duarte* in 1942 and the sensation it caused in Spain. It also began to appear immediately in numerous foreign translations; nothing similar had happened to a Spanish work in many a day. Undoubtedly *Pascual Duarte* marks the revival of the novelistic genre shortly after the close of the Civil War. Some critics have stated that, even before the conflict, the Spanish novel was already in the doldrums; the prestigious critic Julián Marías cites a long list of novelists, some like Azorín and Baroja of the Generation of 1898, who were still writing,[1] but their best literary production was, for the most part, behind them; yet one cannot overlook Cela's debt to the direct, unsentimental style of Baroja. Other novelists of talent before the Civil War found their reputations generally limited to the Spanish-speaking world, with the exception of Vicente Blasco Ibáñez, who, partly because of the movies, became wealthy and famous abroad with *Blood and Sand* and *The Four Horsemen of the Apocalypse*, when he forsook the native regional tradition to write these topical works of passing popularity.

I   *A Contemporary Classic*

After twenty-five years, *La familia de Pascual Duarte* continues to attract attention. The extent of its influence can be measured by the number of articles about it—not all favorable—

31

which are printed, some, in fact, even giving plausible evidence
that it is a bad novel.[2] But a rereading discloses unexpected
facets and the values of a classic, which, indeed, it has become.
Paradoxically, Spain, the land which gave birth to the modern
realistic novel with Don Quijote and the picaresque tales of the
sixteenth and seventeenth centuries, must periodically redis-
cover its own tradition. It is characteristic that Cela studied the
old Spanish authors and was always attracted to the picaresque.

Parallels between Cela and Galdós of the nineteenth century
are worthy of notice. Galdós groped his way, first by assimilating past literature, and gave his country a novel comparable
with those of his contemporaries—Balzac, Dickens, Tolstoy, or
Dostoevski—as is Cela's with that of present-day writers. Simi-
larly, there is in both a detached observation of Spanish life
which may result from their cosmopolitan backgrounds: Galdós
lived his early youth in the Canary Islands among a numerous
English-speaking population, and Cela had a mixed Spanish-
English ancestry. Although different in theme, Galdós' Doña
Perfecta (1886) and La familia de Pascual Duarte (1942)
caused a sensation and marked the emergence of a vigorous
new talent. Both works have been assailed, sometimes from
captious motives: about thirty years ago there was a certain
vogue in pointing out the various defects in Doña Perfecta,[3]
and this has been the case, too, with Pascual Duarte. Yet with
the durability of true classics, both novels occupy a place in
Spanish literary history, although the two authors were destined
to write technically better stories.

The more one examines La familia de Pascual Duarte, the
more one realizes that the deceptively simple autobiographical
narrative of a criminal, at least fifty-five years old, under sentence of death, is more complex than it may at first seem.
There are two preliminary pieces: a "Note of the Transcriber"
and the "Letter Announcing the Posting of the Original Manuscript." In the "Note" Cela presents the fiction of having found
Pascual's memoirs in a pharmacy at Almendralejo which he claims
merely to have transcribed without changing or correcting one
jot or tittle of the original. He does admit to having excised
certain overly crude passages, probably a veiled allusion to the

censorship, and concludes that Pascual is a model of misconduct about whom one can say only: "Do you see what he does? He does just the opposite of what he should" (I, 50).

There follows Pascual's letter to Don Joaquín Barrera López of Mérida, to whom he sends the manuscript because it is a sort of public confession—no small penance in itself—and because Don Joaquín is the only friend of Don Jesús González de la Riva, his last victim, whose address he knows. He hopes that the experiences of his life will prove edifying to someone. Pascual refers to his last crime in such a vague way that quite naturally the reader's interest is aroused.

In a final "Transcriber's Note" at the end of the novel, the author states that this letter, dated Badajoz prison, February 15, 1937, must have been written between Chapters 12 and 13 because of the color of the ink, and that it must have been prepared in advance to produce, in due course, the desired effect, a supposition which would prove that Pascual is not as forgetful or stupid as one may think. Since the simple-hearted murderer would not have such foresight, Cela's statement cleverly serves to conceal that the composition of the first missive is an afterthought on his part.

In Chapter 12, the wife, Lola, is bitter at the death of their second child, and Pascual's hatred for his mother, partly because of her insensitivity to his own mute grief, grows to the extent that he thinks of killing her. The chapter, broken up dramatically by short dialogues and suspension points to indicate the passage of time, ends with the description of how he might kill her while she sleeps. Instead, he decides to flee.

Although he has shown himself capable of violence, up to this time—more than halfway through the novel—Pascual has not committed any crime for which the law has punished him. Earlier, in Chapters 8 and 9, we find him returning from his honeymoon, allowing his wife to go home alone, while he drinks in the tavern, and in a subsequent knife fight wounds Zacarías. When he finally goes home, he learns that his bride, already in an advanced state of pregnancy, has aborted as a result of being thrown by the mare. In a primitive desire for vengeance or perhaps in atonement for his own guilt[4] since he

knew that the mare was skittish (I, 110), he goes to the stable
and stabs the animal at least twenty times. Long before, in
Chapter 1, Pascual, in an impetuous, gratuitous act, has shot
his hunting dog Chispa simply because she "kept looking at me
fixedly, as though she had never seen me before, as if from
one moment to the next she was going to accuse me of something" (I, 64). In Chapter 10 the dog is still alive, and "it seemed
that she looked at me less affectionately" (I, 124). Chispa has
lost three stillborn puppies which she buried in a hole among
the lavender bushes, and when the man and dog go hunting,
the animal "with the sad air of a female without offspring
would approach the hole to sniff at it" (I, 124). Thus the
symbolic connection of the dog with the wife's miscarriage and
his feelings of guilt is explained.

Chapter 12 ends with Pascual's decision to run away to
avoid the recriminations of his wife and mother; there is a
month's interlude in which he writes nothing and decides to ask
for confession from the prison chaplain. With Chapter 13 the
narration goes forward in approximate chronological order. For
two years he stays away from home; on going back, he finds
his wife pregnant by the pimp El Estirao and learns that his
mother has served as go-between in the affair. Curiously, because we should expect his violent nature to rebel earlier, he
has been a long-suffering victim of El Estirao, who has insulted
his manhood and victimized the sister Rosario, for whom
Pascual feels deep affection.

The novel now moves rapidly with mounting tension to its
furious conclusion. When forced, almost brutally, by Pascual to
name the one responsible for her condition, the wife collapses
and dies, evidently from fear. El Estirao comes to take Rosario
away—she has come from the brothel to care for her grieving
brother with great solicitude; the two men fight, and El Estirao
dies at Pascual's hands. For this crime he is of course sent to
prison, but exemplary behavior secures his release after having
served only three years of his sentence. When he returns home,
Rosario has found a new wife for him, and this second marriage
provides him once again a momentary happiness. Yet he finds
that his mother continues to use her "evil arts," and the novel

comes to an abrupt end February 10, 1922, a Friday that year
according to Pascual, when he slays her in her bed after a
terrific struggle.

In 1935 or 1936, possibly in the confusion of the beginning
of the Civil War, Pascual is released from prison a second time.
In a relatively short interval he is back, under sentence of
death for the murder of Don Jesús González de la Riva. Pascual
tells us nothing of his motives for or details of this last crime.
We learn from "Another Note of the Transcriber" that a diligent
search has provided no additional manuscript and that Cela
rejects the thought of filling this lacuna in Pascual's life with a
novelistic tale of his own invention as "a solution repugnant to
the veracity of the book" (I, 196). Such a transparent device
recalls the picaresque novel as well as the manuscript of Cide
Hamete Benengeli, whom Cervantes claimed to be the true
author of *Don Quijote*.

The memoirs end with two letters—one from the prison
chaplain who was with Pascual at his execution, and one from
a corporal of the Civil Guard who was also present and who,
later, delivered the manuscript and letter to Joaquín Barrera
López in Mérida. In his will Don Joaquín leaves his property
to some nuns, with the provision that Pascual's manuscript be
destroyed since it is contrary to public morality and decency
(a reference to the strict Spanish laws only too readily invoked
by an overzealous censorship); but if it survives for eighteen
months, the finder may do as he pleases with it, if such choice
is not contrary to the testator's wishes. This brief legal clause
is placed at the beginning of the novel and, together with all
the other documents, creates an illusion of credibility that reveals to us Cela's narrative skill and artistry.

That the work is sketchy[5] is quite true; yet a criminal like
Pascual might very well write his recollections in just such
desultory fashion—he jumps from beginning to end and end
to beginning, he says, as the ideas occur to him, without stop-
ping to put them in order like a novel (I, 82). For a man who
left school at age twelve, his first-person account discloses an
unusual facility with words. The reader has been accustomed to
overlook this discrepancy ever since the time that unlettered

picaros began recounting their lives in good literary style. Cela breaks up the strict linear order of the traditional novel of the first person and the old structure of the romance where events are strung together, beadlike, one after another. The various accompanying documents, of course, give Pascual's memoirs four perspectives: that of the author, that of the narrator, and those of the two witnesses to his execution.[6] This same technique is used by Cervantes in *Don Quijote* when he presents a series of differing remarks by onlookers at some controversial event and skillfully leads the reader into interesting speculations of his own.

The first half of the book recites in picaresque manner, for the most part with straight-faced irony, the vices of the rogue's parents. Pascual is the offspring of a brutal, drunken Portuguese, who has been in prison, and of a filthy harpy, capable of paying back the husband's beatings in kind, and given to guzzling wine, which she keeps hidden from him. Stricken with rabies, in his final agony the father is kept locked in a closet so as not to frighten the mother into miscarriage. A retarded child is born, who drowns in a vat of olive oil before his tenth birthday. The sister Rosario goes off at age fourteen to become a prostitute. These details are presented with humorlessness and obvious desire to produce a grotesque, macabre effect generally lacking in the picaresque tale. Nor is the picaro ever executed for his misdeeds. Pascual is not a rogue who abandons his family and takes to the open road; rather, except when in prison or during the two-year period of his flight, he is at home with his family, to whom he is linked by bonds that only death can break. Hence the aptness of the title, *The Family of Pascual Duarte*.

II *The Virtuous Murderer*

One should not see the protagonist as the inevitable victim of heredity and environment as in the naturalistic novel, although, upon reading the minute account of the family's degradation, one might be inclined to think so. In the words of one critic, "Provincial life in Spain here lacks the censure of the naturalist and the admiration of the romanticist."[7] There are no naturalistic antecedents for Pascual's crimes: "Pascual has work; his neighbors think well of him; women give themselves to him easily, or so it seems."[8] There is little social protest, never an important element in Cela's writings; only later in life does he develop a deep sympathy for and understanding of country people. Estremadura has regions of impoverished peasants, but this misery is not specified in *La familia de Pascual Duarte*.

The unexplained killing of the wealthy landowner sharpens our curiosity. Besides referring to him in the preface, the criminal dedicates the book to: "The memory of the distinguished patrician Don Jesús González de la Riva, Count of Torremejía, who, when the narrator went to finish him off, smilingly called him 'Pascualillo'" (I, 55). The use of the diminutive suggests friendship, an attitude hardly expected from one on the verge of being murdered. In addition, Pascual does penance on a certain day of the week for this murder. Some scholars have wanted to show that his was a charitable act, performed to prevent Don Jesús from suffering[9] after having been wounded, perhaps, by marauding bands at the beginning of the Civil War. Cela in his final transcriber's note informs us that "it is impossible to verify anything about his activities during the two weeks that the revolution passed through his town, unless we make an exception of the killing of Sr. González de la Riva, to which our protagonist confessed and of which he was convicted" (I, 196); he knows only the bare facts of the case and nothing of the reasons for Pascual's stubborn silence. At the end of the epistle to Don Joaquín Barrera López, the protagonist prays that he "will receive this request for pardon . . . as if it were to Don Jesús himself" (I, 53).

From these lines, then, it would seem that Pascual was guilty of murder, committed perchance as a member of the Republican militia of his home town, which was subsequently defeated when the Nationalist forces of the then Colonel Yagüe Blanco, the Spanish Patton, swept through the region. Rather wearily, Pascual declares in his letter: "I don't want to ask for a pardon, because life has taught me too much evil, and my weakness is too great to resist instinct" (I, 53). Yet the date,

February 15, 1937, while the Civil War was still raging, makes it implausible that he could refer to amnesty for a politically connected crime. Moreover, he considers the writing of his memoirs an act of penance and addresses the manuscript to the only person, to his knowledge, who was acquainted with his last victim.

Even though little space is devoted to Don Jesús González de la Riva, special attention is focused on him by the prominence of his name outside the narrative proper. Within the work itself, there is a brief description of his two-storied house, the only one in town, with its heraldic stone shield over the portal and the many flowers of which he was so fond; he also possessed a country estate near which Pascual hunted. To the non-churchgoing villager, Don Jesús is held up as a model to be imitated in religious ceremonies; therefore, he, as devout Catholic and titled landowner of Estremadura, could have been marked for liquidation by extremist Republicans in 1936. Cela portrays him sympathetically, but, then, neither does he censure Pascual.

Any attempt to solve the enigma of the relationship between murderer and victim leads at best to rather frustrating conjecture and has been considered something of a mare's nest.[10] Some may be irritated that Cela is not more explicit, but for Spanish readers of the period immediately after the Civil War, only the allusion to such an atrocity was sufficient; others will admire his technique of evoking violent death with a minimum of words. The mere sketch of this last crime clearly forms a contrast with the detailed account of matricide, and the variation in tension avoids a ludicrous overdose of violence, a peril that Cela skirts on occasion.

Granted that Pascual is not a psychopathic killer, the opening line of his narration, "I, sir, am not bad, even though I could find reason to be so" (I, 57), may strike the reader as rather broad irony. In the prologue to the third edition of *Pascual Duarte* (1946), Dr. Gregorio Marañón, critic and friend of Cela, makes use of an imaginary dialogue between himself and a young man to argue that Pascual is a good person whose tragedy is to have had almost no way of avoiding being anything but a criminal.[11] His young companion represents the conventional attitude:

Duarte is a bad man, obstinately bad, and it is purely artificial to wish to compare him to heroes who, although bad, always have, even when they stoop to low means, a creative sense and one which is therefore good. (26)

But the older man reminds him that Father Lurueña had found him a " 'gentle lamb, cornered and frightened by life' . . . ," a statement not intended to be taken humorously (26).

In fact, the confessor, like most people, has thought of the prisoner as a hyena until he made his confession. If only the Devil had not at the last moment robbed Pascual of his nerve, "his death might be considered saintly" (I, 198). Father Lurueña's use of the term "cordero" and the name "Pascual" recall the combination "cordero pascual" or sacrificial lamb. His words as he comes forward to be executed, "Let the Lord's will be done," and the name of his victim, Don Jesús, give further emphasis to the idea of sacrifice. Both, then, are martyrs of an unjust society.

The letter from the corporal of the Civil Guard, Cesáreo Martín, touches on the same circumstances, but from a quite different point of view. Pascual has been bearing up well until he develops scruples after confessing for the first time. He fasts on Monday, the day he killed his mother; on Tuesday, the day he killed the Count of Torremejía; on Wednesday because he had killed someone—the guard is not sure whom—so that the wretched fellow spends half the week without eating. When the hour comes for him to be garroted, he comes out with a certain bravado ("flamenco"); at the sight of the gallows he loses all courage and has to be dragged to the execution bench. This account is not entirely incompatible with the "lamb" analogy of the priest, but the taciturn policeman is contemptuous of such an exhibition of cowardice. Cela reports that he can add nothing to what these two men have said. And the reader is left with his questions about Pascual unanswered.

It is evident, however, that Pascual does not die with the courage of a man at peace with God, nor with the perverse but admirable defiance of the hardened criminal or romantic bandit; the recent analogy with the nineteenth-century Argentine outlaw, Martín Fierro, is somewhat far-fetched.[12] Rather, he dies like the poor devil he is. Society has taken its collective vengeance against Pascual, his life for that of the Count of Torremejía. Cela's beliefs (III, 423) echo the arguments against capital punishment.

Marañón believes that the author's truculent style may "prevent our realizing that Pascual is a better person than his victims, and that his criminal excesses represent a sort of abstract and barbarous but undeniable justice."[13] He tends to mythicize the "superhumanly primitive" protagonist and feels that with time this extraordinary biography will be considered as something timeless and exemplary, like the crimes and passions of the old gods (31). Marañón was among the first to judge the novel a classic. Whether or not one agrees, it is undeniable that his remarks have served as a point of departure for numerous critical views.

To say that it is a sophistry for Marañón to judge Pascual's tragedy that "of the man incapable of overcoming by a civilized artifice his instinct for primitive justice"[14] would seem to be mere quibbling. No penal code could redress his very real grievances; Pascual is actually the victim of circumstances beyond his control, and his masculinity and personal sense of justice demand that he take violent action against El Estirao, his mother, and even the horse and dog—although the animals would seem blameless to many. His is the traditional, very Spanish tendency to take justice into one's own hands, to do just what one feels like doing ("hacer la realísima gana").[15] That any of his neighbors would have acted in the same manner is confirmed by the conversation he overhears after his return from prison the first time:

"You see what happened to Pascual."
"And he didn't do a thing that any one of us might not have done."
"Protecting his wife."
"That's right." (I, 178)

While passing criticism often mentions Pascual's primitivism, Paul Ilie, in his study of Cela, develops the concept at some length; but only in the conclusion does he attempt to say precisely what he means: in both Cela and his works the term signifies a tendency to avoid artistic complexity or urban sophistication. So, *La colmena* is not primitive because it is complex and lacks rusticity; but then the critic is led into the fallacy that the themes of hunger and sex in that novel are primitive bonds with Cela's other works, by which statement he evidently means that they are elemental, hence universal, drives. Needless to say, many will not agree with this ultra-refined interpretation.[16] Pascual is brutal but is also capable of tenderness to those who are kind to him; his timidity and emotional immaturity make him incapable of the voluntary giving of affection, and his gentleness "is a primary characteristic of the submissive primitive life."[17] He almost weeps from tenderness toward his wife as she nurses their child, and later is quite solicitous for fear that a "bad air" will carry off the child—hardly a misplaced apprehension since just that misfortune befalls Lola and him. His superstitions, anxieties, strong paternal feelings, and fear of death are elemental emotions, not limited to rural man; they are sufficiently universal to make any reader feel a bond with this countryman in a forgotten, faraway Spanish town. His essential goodness, dejection, and humility are effectively obscured by the pervading spirit of brute force and the cultivated crudity of expression. Ilie agrees that Pascual is not really bad and that he proves it;[18] and another critic, although he finds Pascual not a psychologically coherent person, concurs.[19] Thus we return full circle to Pascual's assertion at the beginning of his memoirs that he is not a bad man.

His sympathy for the stone on which he usually sits when out hunting is not revelatory of a primitive animism, but only of a nostalgia for the familiar things of his former life outside prison walls. Even his sensitivity to the strong odors of farm life is both an example of his nostalgia and a somewhat mild expression of Cela's "tremendismo" to which we must now turn.

III *Tremendismo and Existentialism*

As the term "tremendismo" suggests to those familiar with it, extraordinary crimes at times are portrayed with a wealth of repugnant detail irritating or shocking to those readers who pretend to a certain classical decorum, whatever their literary tastes. Such would be one's impression from reading only *La familia de Pascual Duarte*, but there are "tremendista" elements in other excellent Spanish novels, including Cela's, where murders and suicides are few—an incidental homicide in *La colmena*, a rather grotesque suicide in *Nada (Nothing)*, by Carmen Laforet; often more important is the tone of anguished existence or pessimism.

As early as 1953, in the prologue to *Mrs. Caldwell*, Cela declares: "'Tremendismo' . . . is utterly stupid, a stupidity comparable only to the stupid name given it" (ed. of 1958, p. 10). In *El gallego y su cuadrilla* (ed. of 1955), he tells the story of Zoilo Santisco, a "tremendista" writer pilloried by pharisaical critics and readers, but, alas, it is the only authentic style poor Zoilo has (III, 176-79). Again, in *La rueda de los ocios* (1957) the novelist devotes several pages to demonstrating that the tendency is as old as Spanish literature (ed. of 1962, pp. 13-16). He takes up the cudgels once more in *Papeles*, Number LXXIX, 1962, to point out that 1) he initiated a manner of writing superficially easy to duplicate, and 2) that he has become encumbered by the dead weight of his imitators, a belief that is a personal preoccupation with him (10). When he brought Spanish literature into step with modern European tendencies, he continues, it was with Camus' "fatalism of the absurd" rather than with Sartre's existential anguish, at least in its first moments. "We understand by 'tremendismo' the bloody caricature of reality—not the gory portrait, monstrous and deformed, of an absurd reality." He reiterates that it is as stupid but not as barren as its nickname—a facile term taken up by the press and made into a cliché that will soon become obsolete (10). But the word is pedagogically useful and will be fossilized in histories of literature.

Since Cela stressed the traditional antecedents of "tremendismo," the calling a spade a spade, others have traced these supposed forerunners. Ortega concludes that this literary style has four main characteristics: 1) the tradition of a tendency to unreality, 2) an aversion to a morally or ethically repulsive society, 3) its acceptance by a postwar public used to violence, and 4) an innate pessimism in Cela leading to a re-creation of the ugly aspects of reality to produce an effect.[20] These conclusions, however, do not take enough into account certain widespread contemporary European tendencies, and it is overlooked that many of the passages adduced from Cela show a laconic or harsh treatment of sudden or violent death and sexuality. In earlier literature, with the exception of *La Celestina* (1499), the direct presentation of these two themes is infrequent.

To the average reader the language of "tremendismo" is one generally not voiced, although understood, in polite society. A certain aura of taboo surrounded the literary treatment of particular subjects in the past, but such themes have since become commonplace. In the period after the Civil War, Cela's persistence in demanding the right to say in his works what he pleases is his way of fighting the benighted censorship of his country. He has even been accused of trying to shock his readers so that for this and other reasons his imitators are loath to acknowledge their debt to him. Nevertheless, in post-Civil War Spain and in Europe just after World War II he found a receptive public.

"Tremendismo" has been associated with existentialism. For the moment, let it be said that *La familia de Pascual Duarte* presents a fatalistic acceptance of one's lot that is contrary to the Sartrian concept of freedom. "Tremendismo" complacently accumulates atrocious, horrendous, repulsive, scabrous, and grotesque descriptions,[21] for example, in the details of Pascual's killing of his mother. His hatred for her has grown steadily more intense until one night he takes a kitchen knife and goes to her bedroom. After agonizing hesitation, he is about to abandon his plan when she awakens and calls out, "Who's there?" and he has no recourse other than to carry out his murderous intent.

Pascual has no choice, then, no freedom of action. There is nothing to prevent his running away again from the odious

woman, except that his manhood will not allow it. His thinking
may seem irrational, but his course seems to be foreordained,
if we remember the premonition of matricide at the time of
his previous flight. Their conflict has steadily built up to this
climactic moment.

Then I saw that there was no longer any other solution. I fell upon
her and seized her. She struggled, slipped away. . . . For a moment
she clutched me by the collar. She was shouting like a condemned
soul. We fought; it was the most *tremendous* [italics mine] struggle
that you can imagine. We roared like beasts, spittle drooled from our
mouths. . . . In one of our turnings I saw my wife, white as death,
standing in the doorway without daring to enter. She was holding
an oil lamp in her hand; by its light I could see my mother's face,
purple as the robe of a Holy Week processionist. . . . We kept fighting; my clothes were torn, my chest exposed. The wretched woman
was stronger than the devil. I had to use all my male strength to hold
her down. Fifteen times I had her down, fifteen times she slipped
away. She scratched me, she kicked and beat on me, she bit me. At
one moment she got one of my nipples between her teeth—it was the
left one—and tore it out by the roots. It was the same moment in
which I was able to bury the blade in her throat . . .

Blood spurted out in a torrent and struck me in the face. It was
warm like a belly and tasted the same as the blood of a lamb.

I released her and lit out running. I ran into my wife on leaving;
the oil lamp went out. I got to the fields and ran, ran without resting
for hours. The fields were fresh and a sensation of relief flowed
through my veins.

I could breathe . . . . (I, 193-94)

Those familiar with the violence presented in some American
novels will admit that Cela's description avoids the usual formulas. European authors in the decade following World War
II read the novels of Mike Hammer and James M. Cain as well
as those of more distinguished writers in order to learn how to
portray rough action. Independently Cela hit upon "tremendismo" as an effective way of doing the same thing, a fact that
partly explains his immediate acceptance in foreign circles.

Two more illustrations from *La familia de Pascual Duarte*
lay emphasis upon the shocking brutality and insensitivity of its

characters. When the retarded younger brother, Mario, is four, a hog eats off both his ears. In an effort to console him, neighbor women bring little delicacies during the following weeks, but Mario

. . . spent the days and nights weeping and howling like an abandoned child, and as the slight patience of the mother ran out when most needed, [he] spent months stretched out on the floor, eating whatever was thrown to him, and so dirty that even I who never washed much (why lie about it?) was repelled . . . . (I, 86)

Pascual's narration continues. One day Mario bites Sr. Rafael, now the mother's paramour, on the leg, and the old man kicks the child so hard on one of the scars that he leaves him unconscious, as though dead, and it seems that he will bleed to death. Don Rafael and the mother only laugh. Pascual is frightened to see her so despicable and thinks of picking up the child, but decides not to do so. Later the mother takes the child in her arms and

. . . licked his wound all night like a bitch which had just whelped puppies; the child allowed himself to be loved and even smiled. . . . He went to sleep and on his lips there remained the faint trace of a smile. That night, surely, was the only time in his life that I saw him smile. (I, 86-88)

The incident of the hog and the comparison of the mother to a female dog accentuate the family's bestiality. The scene describing the loss of Mario's ears, so effective at first reading, loses impact when one realizes Cela's lack of logic: hardly would the hog have nipped off so neatly just the ears.[22]

Sometimes Cela's macabre effects contain a certain black humor. In an early short story, "Marcelo Brito" (1941), written while he was also at work on *Pascual Duarte*, there is the description of a child drowned in the millstream.

The body appeared to be caught in the grating of the mill beside a dead chicken which had been there who knows how many days and which never would have been found, if the child of the Portuguese had not drowned; the chicken would slowly have been consumed, slowly dissolved, and the owner would always have had the suspicion that either some neighbor woman or that vagabond with the beard and knapsack who was blamed for everything had stolen it. (II, 68)

So far so good. The reference to the chicken, like that to the hog and bitch, reduces humanity to an elemental level, and, here, demonstrates the absurdity or futility of death. But Cela feels compelled to continue that had the grating not caught the child's body, it might have been milled little by little,

. . . and we would all have eaten it together! . . . Doña Julia—who had a very delicate taste—would perhaps have said, "How strange this bread tastes!" But nobody would have paid any attention to her because we would all have thought that it was one of those peculiar ideas of Doña Julia. . . . (II, 68)

He would have done well to stop with the incident of the dead chicken: bizarre as it is, it fits the pathetic story. But the author could not resist the temptation to try for an added ironic twist. The tale has its own logic, but the reader feels tricked; even if there were no grating, the child's body would not go into the milling room any more than the water does. One understands better Cela's deprecation of the "tremendista" elements of his early literary production; as a conscientious writer, he realizes their lack of authenticity, inevitable perhaps in a young author striving to attract attention.

Because of the widespread European vogue of existentialism, critics have felt it necessary to touch on the possibility of such an influence on Cela's novels, although they have not weighed the matter to any degree. The trend, of course, made itself felt in Spain: at the turn of the century, Unamuno learned Danish in order to read Kierkegaard; Heidegger's *Sein und Zeit* was translated into Spanish in 1933; Ortega spoke of "vital reason" and used the phrase "I am I and my circumstances." One critic declares that if there is a philosophy in Cela's works—a very debatable point—it has to be existentialist since no other can be detected.[23] The parenthetical expression is most significant. Cela cites Malraux, Sartre, and Camus, and privately agrees that

Sartre is pretty much a humbug ("muy farsante") and affirms a high regard for Camus, an admiration repeated frequently in *Papeles*.

A student of Camus points out that the problem of present-day man is his lack of transcendental belief,[24] currently expressed in the "God is dead" discussions. At first sight *La familia de Pascual Duarte* does not reflect any such negative view, but let us reexamine certain aspects. There are priests in the work: the village priest who marries Pascual, and the prison chaplain who answer's Cela's inquiries about the prisoner. In both instances, as well as in "Marcel Brito," the priest is presented in sympathetic if somewhat ironic manner, uttering conventional religious ideas. We recall the prison chaplain's declaration that Pascual would have died a saint if the "enemy" (the devil) had not possessed him at the last moment. The guard, too, admires his fearless words of the first few moments at the appointed time of execution, "Let the Lord's will be done," but then deplores his loss of control. Pascual, in spite of his penance and fasting, never achieves a faith sufficiently strong to sustain him in the face of death. Yet, humble person that he is, the simple "faith of the charcoalburner," so sought after by Unamuno, might plausibly have been his. Cela cannot write an anticlerical or antireligious novel, even in the traditional Spanish sense, in a country where the ecclesiastical hierarchy has just been restored in all its power; but he finds a way to express the agnosticism he shares with other European writers, even as one dramatist attempts to formulate the orthodox answer to Sartre's "No Exit." In the face of the absurd, Pascual is incapable of the leap to faith or of the Christian stoical pose in keeping with the guard's theocentric Spanish viewpoint. Nor can Pascual find that "freedom in death" which comes from losing all illusions as he pits himself against the nothingness of a possible impossibility of existence.[25] Malraux's statement in *Man's Hope*—"The terrible thing about Death is that it transforms life into Destiny," repeated approvingly several times by Sartre in *Being and Nothingness*—is most appropriate for Pascual's despairing surrender to death. He dies as reluctantly as he has lived.

Cela's sympathy for Pascual's dilemma is evidenced in his later references to Meursault of *The Stranger*, which won for Camus the Nobel Prize:

. . . the gratuitous criminal, the man who casts aside consolation and hope and who, facing the "tender indifference of the world," discovers, on the eve of his execution, that the life before which he had always felt an alienation was worth—in spite of everything—the trouble of living it. (*PSA*, no. XX [1957], 116)

For Cela, then, Camus' message is that happiness may be found even in the effort of seeking it in the absurd; this concept leads to charity and compassion, and that of Sartre to nausea and suicide. So, Pascual, like most people, prefers to go on living.

On another occasion Cela quotes from Camus' speech of acceptance for the Nobel Prize: "The writer cannot put himself at the service of those who make history, but, rather, at the service of those who suffer from it," and he agrees that "the novel comes forth from a disobedience of history, as from the disobedience of the angel there sprang the burning fountain of eternal fire" (*PSA*, no. XXIX [1958], 116-17). By history Camus means, of course, Marxist or totalitarian ideologies, but he also does not accept Christian beliefs. And Cela finds it absurd, even stupid, that the automobile accident which took the life of the man who was the conscience of Europe should have been caused by a blowout (*PSA*, no. XLVI [1960], 6).

These remarks show what there was about Camus that appealed most to Cela, but they indicate spiritual affinities rather than direct influences in the earlier-written *Pascual Duarte*. Both Camus and Sartre affirm that the writer, and particularly the novelist, lives in permanent antagonism to conservative forces and that no great novel is reactionary. Cela's novel, however, is not one of social protest. After all, he had just fought for "The Movement," a cause which theoretically was to regenerate Spain. Today such a belief seems, at best, anachronistic; yet another prominent Spanish novelist remarked to me some years ago that the regime could have done so much for economic and agrarian reform had it wished. It seems, then, rather pointless to compare *Pascual Duarte* to *Uncle Tom's Cabin* or *Tobacco Road;* presumably, such comparisons have been proposed because of a vogue in the forties for North American literature.

A certain spiritual tie with the idea of the absurd in *The Stranger* cannot be dismissed so lightly. Hasty critics have wished to imply that somehow Cela must have read the French novel,[26] but the two works of Camus which were to gain him general recognition—*The Stranger* and *The Myth of Sisyphus,* written in 1940 and 1941—were not published until 1942; *Pascual Duarte* was printed in December, 1942, but Cela had read selections from it to friends at the Café Gijón as early as 1940 and had finished the manuscript January 6, 1942. It took him the rest of the year to find a printer. Yet there are parallels between the two works.

According to Cruickshank,[27] the literature of revolt has three main characteristics. First, there is a blurred distinction between good and evil, right and wrong. Marañón's preface points out that Pascual is not evil, although his young interlocutor is right, from a conventional legal and moral point of view, in asserting that he is bad. In *The Stranger,* Meursault shows no emotion at his mother's death and burial, a shocking indifference in a society that reveres, however hypocritically, home and mother. Pascual's reflections prior to matricide show an attitude more typical of filial hostility toward a parent:

I didn't dare, after all she was my mother, the woman who had borne me, and whom, for that reason, I had to pardon. . . . No, I couldn't pardon her because she had borne me. By thrusting me into the world, she had done me no favor, absolutely none . . . . (I, 192)

The last line recalls the Nietzschean existentialist feeling of being "thrown into the world."[28]

Second, the existentialist novel emphasizes concrete situations rather than abstract attitudes. Pascual, like Meursault, always refuses to say more than he feels and is not concerned with abstractions; Camus points out this trait in his protagonist. While Pascual presumably confesses and even does penance, little contrition appears in his narrative. *The Stranger,* virtually an anti-novel in comparison with the classics of the past century, has a laconic, anti-rhetorical style and a preoccupation with material objects rather than ideal essences such as Beauty, Truth, Goodness, Glory, and Honor. Cela's novel has perhaps a bit more coherence, but Pascual, like Meursault, lacks the traditional lucidity and omniscience of the first-person narrator, who, in reality, is more akin to the all-knowing third-person storyteller. Both works display a non-analytical vocabulary and show a high degree of self-consciousness in the use of words, particularly so in the case of Camus—a trait presumably that of the absurdist writer. Cela's vocabulary retains more of the traditional richness of the Spanish realistic novel, whereas Camus admits to a considerable influence, at this stage, of the "tough" American novelists such as Faulkner and Steinbeck.

Characterization is alien to the absurdist novel; events lack an orderly pattern, and character analysis and plot construction are regarded with suspicion. Cela has been criticized for a lack of character portrayal.[29] But he hardly needed foreign models for this tendency. Early in the twentieth century, while still possessing followers of the realistic, "costumbrista" tradition, the Spanish novel is radically modified by Unamuno, primarily concerned with expressing his metaphysical anguish and doubt at the expense of plot and psychological depth; by Azorín, with his impressionistic, aesthetic approach, stressing the "eternal recurrence"; and by Baroja, unpreoccupied with his simple, direct style, who states that novels do not need plots since life is plotless and unfolds as one lives it. This is not to say, all the same, that Cela reflects any particular influence of these writers, especially in *La familia de Pascual Duarte.*

The third important aspect of the literature of absolute revolt shows the individual bereft of metaphysical aids, the insistence on the fact of human responsibility. We have seen that spiritual help fails Pascual when he is faced with the fact of his execution; he tends to fatalistic resignation and does not exhibit that freedom of choice available to the existentialist hero.[30] Far from being indifferent like Meursault, Pascual has conflicts within himself and with others motivated by hatred; he also has moments of conformity and revolt which distinguish

him to some degree from the passive rebel Meursault. Because
of his existentialist philosophy, Meursault, unlike Pascual, is
above any discussion of good and evil. Regarded by many
Spaniards as a heterodoxy at the very least, existentialism is
replaced in Spain, according to Julián Marías,[31] by the tragic
sense of life of Unamuno and Ortega. When Sartre's philosophy
was most in vogue, government censorship would hardly have
allowed such writings to circulate freely. A brutal or senseless
crime is still called by the Spanish press a "crimen existencialista."

This brief discussion was certainly not undertaken to force
Cela into an existentialist mold. There are only a few circumstantial, thematic similarities between *Pascual Duarte* and *The
Stranger*. Both are short first-person narrations, written in a
simple, suggestive style. There are casual parallels: Meursault
possesses Marie immediately after his mother's death, and
Pascual deflowers Lola on the grave of the just-buried Mario.
Then come the final incarceration—after three murders by
Pascual, only one by Meursault—repentence or indifference,
and, ultimately, the confession.[32] Furthermore, Pascual is not a
twenty- to thirty-year-old man like Meursault; on the first page
of his memoirs he states that he was born over fifty-five years
before.

CHAPTER 3

A New Technique

SHORTLY after his second stay in a tuberculosis sanitarium, Cela published *Pabellón de reposo* (1943), translated into English with the rather inaccurate title *Rest Home*. No doubt his emotions and preoccupations as a patient contributed greatly to the elaboration of the novel. He states in the prologue that the work contains "much—even more than much—of my personal experiences and no little imaginary anecdote, perhaps it would be better to say: situation" (I, 206). From reality he went on to derive a literary presentation. When reading the novel, one should bear this statement in mind so as not to identify any single character or attitude with that of the author. In fact, possibly all seven inmates reflect at times his reactions and feelings, and for this reason their personalities remain rather nebulous; of course, there are also technical reasons, some deliberate—for example, the patients are known only by their room numbers and each is given a rather brief, parallel role in the two parts of the book. *Pabellón* has been compared to *The Magic Mountain*, evidently because certain details recall the chapter title "Number 34" of Thomas Mann's work. The scope and general outlook of the two novels are quite different, but from it Cela may have received a preliminary impetus for writing this sort of very personal account. A more lyrical parallel is Clarín's story, "El dúo de la tos" ("The Coughing Duet"), 1896, about a lonely, tubercular woman and man in rooms 32 and 36 of a large hotel and the night they spend coughing. Number 36 goes his way the following day, soon to die, and 32 lives only two or three years.

I *An Anti-Pascual*

In *Pabellón,* there is an impression of concreteness which
contrasts sharply with *La familia de Pascual Duarte.* As he announces in the prologue to *Mrs. Caldwell habla con su hijo*
(1953), he tries to create here an anti-Pascual. To answer one
critic who wished to see him treat a static theme and situation,
an idea that he does not understand very well, he "wrote
Pabellón de reposo, which is a novel where nothing happens
and where there are no blows, murders, turbulent love, and
only the minimum of blood necessary so that the reader will not
feel deceived and think the tuberculosis patients are rheumatics
or syphilitics." He calls it his "peaceful experiment," his second
approach to the novel (10-11). Robert Kirsner stresses the
symbolism of blood in the work, and though he may have over-
emphasized his claim that it is really a case of the *Pascual*
raised to the realm of calm poetry, which only heightens the
horror of it all, one is inclined to agree.[1] And, clearly, a book
in which seven people, afflicted with tuberculosis, inexorably
die can hardly be said to be a novel in which "nothing happens."
The reader feels an added poignancy not envisioned by Cela
when he realizes that within a few years, thanks to antibiotics,
tuberculosis will have become a largely curable disease.

Of special significance is the rigidly symmetrical structure.[2]
Each of the two parts contains seven chapters that correspond
to the seven main characters. The first part is followed by an
interlude, the second by an epilogue. The personages alternate
in order of appearance according to sex: male, female, male. If
one has an interior monologue in Part I, he has a corresponding
recital in Part II. Number 37 records twelve days in her diary,
covering the same days of the week in two chapters of the two
parts. Character 2 writes eight letters, one for each day, from
Sunday to Sunday, the two times he appears. The author interrupts his narration in the sixth chapter of each part to make
observations on the implications of the work.

This symmetry is of course not too obvious. Its real purpose
is to provide a sense of order for an accumulation of apparently
random sentiments, impressions, and emotions. Cela published

the novel first in the weekly *El Español*; one is a bit skeptical of the statement in his latest prologue that "it is not a difficult novel nor one of complex technique and it was possible for me to go along writing it each week without any particular effort" (I, 207). He claims to have watered down his observations on the meanness, baseness, and violence of sanitarium life that unfolded before his astonished eyes; by thus emphasizing the supposed veracity of the account, he may possibly combat unfavorable criticism for exaggeration or "tremendismo."

Additional structural analysis is needed. The characters are endowed with sufficient personality so that one can say, as does Castellet[3]: Number 52 is a university student (actually he has just graduated), 37 a young girl, 14 a poet, 40 a coquette, 11 a young man in love with a sweetheart on the outside to whom he writes, 103 a dreamy woman, and 2 a banker and investor. So that the reader may be cognizant of their subtle interrelationships, first-person narrations without explanations reveal their activities, plans, hopes, and fears. Chapter I presents the reaction of Number 52 to his personal situation and his concern for Number 37. The following clinical detail is characteristic of Cela's procedure:

She always tells me, almost mysteriously, her sad afflictions. She says to me, for example:
"Yesterday, do you know I had three large bloody sputums and five small ones? Don't you think, surely, that it must have come from the throat?" (I, 221)

The second chapter finds Number 37 writing in her diary about her growing intimacy with Number 52 and of his frequent visits to her. As it happens, she makes rather premature mention of the death of Number 14 because there is a detailed presentation in Part II where all die. While the second part relates the deaths of the seven patients in the same order in which they appear in the first, the author does not mean to imply that this is the real sequence of events. Number 14's unpleasant, still very fresh memories of preparatory school probably are a reflection of Cela's joyless recollections; but 14 also describes the death of his beloved mother, while the author's is still very much alive. Hence, there is Cela's typical fusion of autobiographical and imaginary elements. This mother is, in all major ways, just the opposite of Pascual's, a fact which reminds us again of Cela's intention of writing an "anti-Pascual."

According to the pattern that has now developed, a woman, Number 40, takes up the narration. She refers occasionally to Number 14 toward whom she feels ". . . romantic and maternal. . . . What a paradox!" (I, 242), a statement which makes a connection with the previously detailed description of Number 14's loss of his mother. Number 40, a woman of the world, yearns for the gay social gatherings of evening; when the distant lights of Madrid come on, she recalls past family soirées with nostalgia. Although the lights are visible to those in this sanitarium in the mountains, the capital is now a remote world.

Number 40 also gives a description of the cart which at twilight had come to carry away the body of the former patient assigned her same number. This verbal picture is a good example of Cela's lyricism, which appears occasionally even in *La familia de Pascual Duarte*, and for this reason, as well as for the fact that it becomes a key symbol of death in Part II, it is presented in detail:

The little cart was going along the path between the pines, bordering the ravine, approaching close to the stream in which the moon was reflected, cold and impassible like the image of death itself. The gardener was pushing it, the red-haired gardener, who sings in a low voice when he trims the geraniums and roses, was pushing it.

When he goes up the hill, he says, "Gee up!" and the little cart, with its iron wheel bounding over the small boulders, responds with the shrill squeak of an axle in need of grease, and afterwards it is lost from sight, bouncing from rock to rock, as it climbs upward. When it goes along the smooth road of the stream, where ferns and maidenhairs display their greenness along the banks and where the soft moss and white lichens seek the damp bark of the oaks in order to live, the gardener, as though intoxicated by that peace, half sings, as always, his affectionate and musing song.

The little cart is made of iron, with a single wheel. In times past it was painted green, a brilliant emerald green color, but now it is

already old, already subdued, already sad and colorless. Appropriate
for the use to which it is put!

Across the little cart, sticking out from the sides, appears the coffin,
among the shadows of the night, like an old evergreen oak leveled by
a bolt of lightning.

And inside a dead man . . . . (I, 240-41)

If the reader detects poetic influences of García Lorca in the
simile of the moon as a symbol of death, it is because this picture
of the burial of the first Number 40 is an expression of the
sentiments of the young poet, Number 14. The gardener pruning
the geraniums and roses is a literal suggestion of the Grim
Reaper. That to the worldly Number 40 the boy poet seems a
"beautiful and fresh romantic daguerreotype" (I, 241) enables
Cela not only to indulge in this fanciful, evocative flight, but
also to justify a frank prospect of romance for the two. But in
spite of her admiration for the boy, she prefers the more mature
man of the world.

Her rather superficial observations enable us to envision certain other patients more clearly. The boy poet is destined for
"angelical girls, timid young things . . . like poor, resigned 37,
who is a beautiful Virgin Mary without a child to cradle in her
arms" (I, 241). Number 40 belittles the girl because she does
not use makeup. If 37 did not suffer from a natural reticence,
she would appeal to the amorous nature of the young 14.
Number 40's powers of observation are, however, limited. She
believes that 37 detests Number 52 (I, 242), and Cela's delicate
irony is not lost on the reader, who knows that the girl and the
more mature man, in reality, are attracted to each other. Number
40 also has qualities of the eternally feminine matchmaker.

For an understanding of Part II of the novel, the three re-
maining characters must be briefly identified. For each there
is a corresponding chapter. Thus, Chapter V reveals three
letters Number 11 writes on Monday, Tuesday, and Wednesday,
signing himself "C." In Part II he will write three letters to his
sweetheart outside the sanitarium, although the last will be
interrupted when death "threw away the pen from [his] bony
hand . . ." (I, 333). Chapter VI introduces Number 103, who is
dreaming of Number 73, a seaman—evidently a former patient—

who has died in his own home. She copies his letter from Port of Spain, Trinidad, in which he states that her reply was never received. It is returned to her only a few hours after she reads of his death in the local newspaper.

The author interrupts, as he will do again in Chapter VI of Part II, to insert a message from his friend Dr. A. M. S. pleading that he suspend the series because of the depressing effect on his tubercular patients. Such letters heighten the illusion of reality as successfully here as in *La familia de Pascual Duarte*. Cela affirms that his personages are purely fictitious and that nobody should identify with them (I, 267), all the while knowing from personal experience and observation of human nature that just the opposite reaction will occur. Paradoxically, real tubercular sufferers might be less affected than the average healthy reader, who would imagine all kinds of symptoms.

Chapter VII contains a series of letters written by Number 2, signed "B," a banker and speculator who, at first, is highly optimistic that he will soon be back doing business as usual. He gives orders about what stocks to buy and sell, how to arrange the affairs of his mistress Fifi, the allowance to be made to his estranged wife, and requests that the public be told he is on a business trip to Damascus or Cairo. Gradually he becomes less concerned with the material world and more preoccupied with thoughts of his wife and school-age daughter. As he realizes little by little that it may take years for his recovery, he thinks of a reconciliation with his wife and then, unexpectedly, declares himself to be mildly happy. Friends are still not to be informed; it is ridiculous for a banker to die in such a manner. In his last letter come the phrases to be of so much importance at the end of the book: "The divine plan, God—do you realize, my friend, that God is a more tangible reality than the dollar, the pound sterling, than oil wells?" (I, 277-78).

In the "Interlude" at the end of Part I, Cela presents the board meeting of the directors of the sanitarium, giving statistics on incoming patients, deaths, partial and complete cures. The number of the deceased totals fifty-two, and the cures, partial and complete, fourteen. Then the young resident doctor pro-

poses additional investments which will be amortized in eight
to ten years and will provide an income "at least as good as that
of the healthiest business" (I, 280). The scene shifts to the
sewing room of the nurses' quarters. One nurse, entering to
change her bloody uniform, is laughing at the absurd spectacle
of the patient who has just died: in his final spasms he kicked
off all the covers and appeared stark naked, bathed in blood,
wearing only his socks and garters (I, 281). Then we are introduced to the kitchen and the hospital cook, so envied by Number
52 at the beginning because of his perfectly normal good health;
he has a large belly and a touch of rheumatism. Cela gives
details of the bustling activities of the chambermaid with her
eternal smile, who is only occasionally reminded of the horrify-
ing, real condition of the patients (I, 222). In the final episodes
we learn of the cook's involvement in a vulgar affair with the
pregnant scullery maid, and of ordinary matters in the lives
of people on the outside. The obvious purpose of these vignettes
is to bring into bold relief the desperate plight of the inmates
and to stress the fact of the segregation of these given-up-for-
dead from the world of the living, an illusion increased by the
glow of lights from the distant city. In spite of their tentative
friendships, they are isolated from one another by their preoccupation with their own ill health to the extent that each
sits in solitude awaiting the end.

II *The Death Cart*

In Part II of *Pabellón de reposo* the characters appear in the
same order as before and die one by one, but the deaths are
not narrated in a strictly chronological order. So, in Chapter I,
Number 52 soliloquizes about the death of 37, who is still alive
in Chapter II. Four lines of the lyrical "The little cart goes along
the path between the pines . . ." indicate his death at the end of
Chapter I. The cart of course bears the dead to the cemetery.
Not only is Number 37 still alive in the next chapter, but she
narrates pathetically in her diary details of 52's visits; nevertheless, her demise is indicated, too, by succeeding lines from the
lyric. And so it goes.

The author interrupts the first-person narration of Number 103, who is dreaming of her sailor sweetheart, now six months dead, with a letter from a patient—and childhood English friend into the bargain—asking, just as the Doctor of Part I has done, that he suspend publication of his accounts of sanitarium life. He provides authentic autobiographical references to heighten the apparent veracity of his recital, even including a letter in picturesque Anglicized Spanish from his great-aunt, Katherine Trulock, who has brought the old friend into contact with him again. Cela protests that if he felt that his work was truly pernicious, he would gladly stop writing; he affirms that if his novel were read with insight, it could even provoke optimism because those he presents, besides being fictitious persons, are tubercular and know better than anyone else that they are representatives of an existence to be avoided like fire as a first step by those seeking a cure (I, 343-44). The statement is so ambiguous that it is really double talk. Critics unfavorable to Cela have noted his tendency to become involved in noisy polemics; here one suspects him of inventing a controversy that does not exist. Yet, as a part of the structure of the work, its inclusion is quite justified since it injects a note of reality from the outside world to contrast with the rarefied atmosphere of the hospital. One is returned with dramatic effectiveness to the patients' world when the interrupted Number 103 resumes her narration for a few lines, ending "If I die without continuing my account . . ." (I, 345). A row of suspension points indicates the passage of time, followed by the now familiar refrain with lines about the red-haired gardener and the cart. This almost nostalgically lyric suggestion of death is much more moving than gruesome details could be.

The flight of time provides additional unity for the story. At the beginning it is early June and now, at the end, the first few days of November have arrived. Some of Cela's most poetic lines have to do with the passing of these four months. Chapter I tells us that in early July the cattle are leaving the hot, dry lower pastures for those up in the mountains and that the locusts are singing among the thistles (I, 211); this is not imagery of an original sort, but the season is succinctly evoked by a symbol

universally recognized in countries of temperate climate. At the
end, after all have died, the cattle are returning to escape the
mountain snows of early November and the locusts no longer
sing among the thistles (I, 353).

In Chapter II of the first part there is sufficient reference to
the summer heat to lay stress upon the season; in the second
part the melancholy of autumn provides an effective mood for
the coming of death. The season of the nightingale, the time of
the warm, calm days, gives way to fall:

Autumn is a bad season. The leaves of the trees fall inexorably, like
a summons, from stems hardened by rain and wind, and the ground
is carpeted with a thick layer of foliage which displays all the shades
of death: the yellow of canaries, of lemons, wheat, ocher which is so
pleasing to the sight, sienna which makes us tremble . . . . (I, 289-90)

In general, the patients' attitudes toward God show sincere
belief, but theirs is not a conventional death; no priest attends
them to offer consolation or to administer the last rites, and
their bodies are unceremoniously removed to the cemetery
in the little cart. This lack may first seem to be an oversight
on the author's part since priests are included in La familia de
Pascual Duarte; but the omission is deliberate—all external
complicating religious practices contrary to the unity of the work
are eliminated. Such ceremony, logically a part of the realistic
novel, is commonly rejected by modern cultivators of the genre,
whether Camus or Unamuno.

Number 11 cries out in a letter to his sweetheart, "God exists,
my beloved, but He is not on our side. Can we go on with
confidence?" (I, 330). This concept of deistic indifference is re-
futed with a wry twist at the end of Chapter V when the
sweetheart writes him a cruel letter brusquely breaking off their
relationship: she has no intention of "embarking on a sinking
ship. If once I loved you, forget it. Regards, A." However, "this
letter was returned to the sender; it had arrived too late. There
is no doubt that God arranges matters wisely" (I, 333-34).

Each personage has an individual approach to God. Number
52, for instance, mourning the death of 37, tends to think of

Him as a sort of summum bonum with a tinge of paganism when he questions whether the unfortunate woman can be really happy in heaven since she has never, even for a moment, known the joy of a healthy body. For several pages more 52 rails against God for allowing mankind to suffer so much (I, 288-95). Number 37 laments in turn that God has cursed her, marked her (I, 300); and the young poet, in hope of consolation from Thomas à Kempis, feels guilty of contempt for God because of his resistance to death and cries out—an echo of Unamuno—that blasphemy may be "the most frightened prayer, the last shout that God receives in His praise. Hatred is the love of the person who is despised" (I, 312).

The final Christian message is contained in the account of the peaceful, resigned death of the businessman. He realizes that his condition is worsening, but exclaims, "I am so happy!" (I, 346). All former preoccupation with material gain is dismissed as trivial, his last thoughts express gratitude to the friend for aid to his wife and daughter, and he leaves him the pen with which he is writing, for ". . . with it I earned a lot of money, but don't forget that with it I have also written the only sincere words of my life" (I, 351). This stoical, cheerful attitude toward death contrasts so strongly with Pascual Duarte's failure to die "a good death" that we believe more than ever the author's intention of writing an anti-Pascual novel.

CHAPTER 4

A Yearning for the Open Road

IN 1944 Cela again demonstrates his versatility as a writer
with *Nuevas andanzas y desventuras de Lazarillo de Tormes*
—the rather cumbersome title parallels that of the original
Lazarillo—partly in answer to critics whom he wished to give
proof of his ability to write a novel with a local Spanish setting,
rather than an abstract one that could be located anywhere.
In further remarks in the prologue to *Mrs. Caldwell habla con
su hijo,* he notes that he was attracted to "one of the oldest,
most beautiful, and illustrious myths of our classical literature,
that of the servant with a hundred masters, the rogue who lives
by a miracle and even by pure chance" (11-12). His emphasis
on the aesthetic value of the picaresque genre should be borne
in mind by those who like to see in this type of novel social
criticism or literature of protest.[1] Nineteenth- and twentieth-
century critics have been unable to escape a pruritis to equate
the genre with Spain's decadence in the sixteenth century and,
particularly, the seventeenth, and Marxist critics find it a reprehensible example of rising bourgeois tastes;[2] while there may
be some portrayal of customs, social satire, and a semblance of
objectivity, one must agree with Cossío when he says in the
prologue to Cela's novel that reality in picaresque literature
is as deformed as in the pastoral and the Moorish tale so popular
in their time.[3]

I   An Eternal Genre

Today, like the novels of chivalry, the pastoral and the
Moorish tale are dead, but the tradition initiated in 1554 with

Lazarillo de Tormes is very much alive. With the introduction
of the youthful picaro and his at times cynical, at times artless
narration of the antics of all social types, modern humanity
entered fully into literature; the autobiographical tale, so common today, was then a daring innovation.[4] It is unfortunate
that Auerbach, in his study of the portrayal of fictional reality
in *Mimesis,* did not examine a portion of one of the great
Spanish picaresque novels. This new trend, incorporating older
realistic elements such as those in *The Book of Good Love* by
Juan Ruiz and *The Celestina,* in the middle of the fourteenth
and at the end of the fifteenth centuries respectively, gave a
direction to Spanish literature that influenced greatly the realistic
novel of France and especially England of the eighteenth century, and still has vitality today.

The important concern is of course that Cela is returning to
a fundamental tradition. Again in the prologue to *Mrs. Caldwell*
(11), he states that in a book such as his *Lazarillo* one is always
on the verge of creating a pastiche, but at the same time one
learns something useful. In his latest prologue to the book he admits that his purpose was to acquire a Castilian language rooted
in the people, based on the spoken, not the written language,
which could serve as a tool for his purposes (I, 357). The
problem was to decide whether prose was to be an instrument
for literary expression or an end in itself, with his final choice
in favor of the first approach; implied is a reiteration of his
belief that aesthetic preoccupations lead to sterility. Hence, his
Lazarillo is a turning point at a critical time in his career. The
sixteenth-century classic is not only a model, but an inspiration,
"a marvel of charm and simplicity." For this reason, then, he
regards his version of the novel with gratitude and love (I,
358-60).

One good quality which even the longest and preachiest of
the later picaresque novels always possess is the portrayal of
the main protagonist in widely varied situations. Seldom is an
anecdote or adventure repeated. So, Cela is successful in finding new incidents and types with which to associate his hero.
There is a rather daring novelty right at the beginning: Lázaro
—typically the son of a promiscuous mother—is abandoned to

some shepherds after being nursed only two weeks; his first memory is that of being suckled by a she-goat. As a reader of Gracián, Cela may have recalled that Andrenio in *El criticón (The Critic)*, was nursed by a wild animal, but of unspecified kind. The hero indulges in a series of cynical observations as to which of several men might have been his father, a situation permitting a display of considerable bawdy humor. The unedifying ancestry of the picaro is conventional, but never do the first rogues take to the highway until they are of an age to serve a master. At the outset, then, Cela imposes his originality on the genre and, in the process, captures the reader's attention with his story of the forsaken infant.

Critics have seen in Cela's *Lazarillo* a preview of the series of books about excursions to various regions of Spain that he will write in later years. In fact, *Lazarillo* has been discussed in a preliminary study of editions of these travel accounts.[5] It is true that this tale probably shows an early interest in the possibility of peregrinations through the Spanish countryside, but the later accounts are factual in presentation while his *Lazarillo* is a purely literary creation. Such episodes as he includes in the work could happen only in fiction. For example, Lázaro falls in with three bizarre wandering musicians. Outside an inn a young man, Julian, approaches asking alms because his father has abandoned him. The grief of the nearly grown boy, his remarks about cowardly townspeople, and unflattering allusions to his parents surprise the wanderers. By then the eyes of Lázaro and his companions have grown accustomed to the darkness of the interior and they see the father and stepmother hanging from a beam. The boy adds that there are more upstairs; and, indeed, the search party finds two servant girls also suspended. They seize the mad boy and tie him up; when the townspeople return armed, the boy begins to rave, tremble, and foam at the mouth, whereupon those already in the patio run around in cowardly fashion and those outside bombard the house with bullets and stones from slings. The boy dies from his malady, not, ironically, from the furious onslaught of the villagers. To celebrate, the people take down from their chimneys all kinds of hams, sausages, and other cured meats in

preparation for a big feast. The implied analogy with the
taking down of the hanged family is typical of Cela's sardonic,
truculent humor, the effect of which is heightened by Lázaro's
remark: ". . . at least for the time being we all came out ahead
and well fed" (I, 396).

In most of his writings Cela is compassionate, an aspect that
should be stressed since a saturnine exterior has often caused
his innate sensitivity to be overlooked. His own accounts of his
childhood reveal an impressionable boy, and it is likely that
his brusque personality traits are a defensive façade. Those who
know him well claim that he is essentially a timid person. At
times he is the victim of the image that he himself helped to
create. A Spanish lady who, as member of a group, met him
at the airport in New York City in January, 1964, later reported
in a Barcelona newspaper that he was unusually well behaved
that day. Needless to say, Cela was quite perplexed by the
newspaper account. One suspects that the public at times expects his behavior to compare with that of the characters in his
novels.

II *Altruism and Actuality*

The compassion that is a fundamental ingredient of Cela's
work is conveyed sometimes by the contrast with the portrayal
of accentuated brutality or grotesqueness. The sympathy evinced
for the crazy mass murderer is momentary but no less sincere:

Poor Julian appeared dead and thoroughly beaten, but the coroner
said, when he performed the autopsy, that all of the blows and knife
wounds had been inflicted after he was a cadaver. It is better thus.
(I, 395)

After this incident, the musicians abandon Lázaro. He then
meets a man "so thin that he appeared the very mirror of death
or a messenger of hunger" (I, 404), seated on a stone by the
river Yeltes delousing himself. Readers of Spanish picaresque
novels will note the underlying style of Quevedo in this phrase.
The man so described, who calls himself the Penitent Philip, is
"one of the only two good persons I ever met in all my days"

(I, 425), the grief-stricken Lázaro says later, at the time of Philip's death. Philip is crackbrained and often imagines that he sees new stars in the skies, with the result that scientific people laugh at him; he is possibly symbolic of a sort of poetic, idealistic vision of the cosmos. The boy is frightened one day when his master speaks of the transmigration of souls and does not know how to reply. The master's response is significant: "You already know enough just by existing" (I, 409).

His meaning is that Lázaro may have in him the soul of a saint, wise man, or some famous ancient warrior. Philip then tells of a rooster in the town who is the reincarnation of a former prosecuting attorney and provincial deputy, and who knows the fate in store for him will inevitably be the frying pan—a recollection of the Pythagorean rooster which met a similar fate in the sixteenth-century *Crotalón* of Cristóbal de Villalón. Cela has recently remarked slyly that he once said he believed in metempsychosis, but that it is not true (II, 541).

Somewhat later the wanderers encounter Philip's mad wife from whom they escape by swimming a stream, a graphic illustration of the master's valuable suggestion always to stay near rivers. Cold and wet, the Penitent Philip and Lázaro next meet a gamekeeper who advises the boy that unless he becomes wiser he will often go hungry. The irony is that he has already stolen a cooked partridge from the keeper's knapsack. Such words of advice are also foolish in Lázaro's opinion, because in order to eat all one has to do is keep moving. Townspeople will give food to a vagabond and abuse one of their own:

. . . they are so cruel that if he is hungry, they call him an idler; if he has no sense, they throw stones at him with the result that in every Spanish town there is a man, mere skin and bones, whom boys stone, women call a fool, and men say that all he wants is to live without working. (I, 418-19)

But Cela does not stop there. He has Lázaro go on at great length about one of these "innocents" he has known and the terrible sport people made of him. In the brief prologue to *Mis páginas preferidas (My Favorite Pages)*, Cela informs us that he chose this chapter for the anthology "perhaps because my poor friend the Penitent Philip is particularly congenial to me" (I, 597).

Soon thereafter Lázaro falls in with a group of French acrobats who have a small traveling show, which includes a tame bear, a poodle, and a trembling, half-bald monkey. Nothing indicates more clearly the brutality of the troupe than the account of the death of the monkey: "Poor Pompadour died a little while after I joined the French, and I prefer to forget the things they said to her and the kicks they gave the body" (I, 440). Sad, unfortunate Marie is another victim of her companions' cruelty. As she sits rocking a child, she engages Lázaro in this conversation, the most touching in the book:

"Couldn't you raise the child?"
Señorita Marie looked like an angel filled with sadness. With a bitter voice she murmured.
"No, the child isn't mine. Although you may not believe it, I am a virgin."
Señorita Marie sighed.
"Nobody loves me."
I felt like telling her that I loved her . . . , but I remained silent.
"The child is Violette's; she had three at one time . . . "
There was a catch in her voice, and her eyes were closed.
"She didn't want this one, because it was born blind."
I covered my face with my hands. My eyes were moist, I couldn't help it.
"She wanted to throw it out, and I asked her for it. I love it as though it were mine . . . "
It was as though a heavy weight were pressing down upon us. I tried to change the conversation.
"And Señor Etienne doesn't love you?"
"Etienne is my brother. He is two years older than I. The poor fellow is good but given to vice . . . "
"I thought he was your husband."
"Yes, everybody thinks that. Sometimes he thinks so too. . . . " (I, 445)

This scene has an agreeable sequel when Lázaro and Señorita Marie with the child, the bear Ragusain, and the poodle Colosse

take refuge in the home of the eccentric squire and poet Don
Federico, doubtless the other one of the "only two really good
men" the vagabond claims to have met in his travels. Cela has
introduced a modern sentimental note, which one finds only
rarely in the classical picaresque novel. There is no denying
the attraction of the original *Lazarillo de Tormes* and the sympathy one feels for the boy, but the anonymous author narrates
dispassionately and cynically, rarely with compassion. Not until
*Periquillo el de las gallineras (Little Peter of the Lady Poul-
terers)* by Francisco Santos in 1668 does one find in somewhat
greater number those elements which will appear in the sentimental novel of the next century. Of course, the tender heart
under the rough exterior is also typical of Hemingway and the
"tough" modern writers.

While the picaresque tale is only an apparent portrayal of
reality, there is no doubt that it provides the author an opportunity to give expression to his vision of the world. Since
Cela admits that he dons various masks, one must take care
not to regard certain passages as a voicing of his personal attitudes; yet there are incidents of a self-revelatory nature which
furnish him the occasion for satire of some benighted outlook,
such as that favorite bugbear of the reactionary Spanish clergy—
Freemasonry.

Some time later I was told by a friend of mine, who was the proprietor of a shop selling candles and rosaries in Talavera de la Reina
and who went by the name of Filemón Frayle, that in France everybody was a Mason and an Enemy of pious habits. . . . Don Filemón
was an educated and unprejudiced man and what he said was almost
always true. (I, 442)

Here Cela presents his satire in the naive words of the picaro,
and, just to be sure that the point is not missed, he calls the
storekeeper Frayle (friar).

After he leaves the service of Don Federico, Lázaro travels
for several days until he finds himself looking down from the
mountains over the plain of La Mancha. The vagabond thinks
briefly of settling in one of the places spread out before him:

At my feet were to be seen the towns set out as though by hand, and before deciding which should be mine, I looked at them calmly, like the lord of all he surveys, amusing myself by imagining them as fertile and friendly as, to my misfortune, none of them was, and I thought of them orderly and prosperous as, to the misfortune of their inhabitants, not a single one turned out to be.

I looked to the East and saw wretched towns in ruins and miserable villages with beautiful names. In the distance Palomares del Campo squatted on the earth as though afraid, and Torrejoncillo del Rey was perishing among the fallow fields like a thirsty animal. Nearer to the mountains the Gigüela flowed through its hard bed of stones, and Horcajada de la Torre and Villanueva de los Escuderos looked startled at their old and wrinkled grimaces in the scanty water. I saw that they were the towns of those who had come down in the world and I turned my back on them; times were hard, and a slice of bread was easily worth ten armorial stone shields. (I, 466-67)

The last few words refer to the heraldic arms emblazoned over the doorways of the decaying old family mansions. Here it is evident that the author has caught something of the timelessness of rural Spain sleeping in its misery. Spanish writers of the Generation of 1898 were conscious of this eternal Spain, but they seldom expressed themselves with this peculiar bitterness. Conditions were particularly grim during this post-Civil War period. Cela's view is reminiscent of the pessimism of Mateo Alemán in *Guzmán de Alfarache*, and Lázaro's almost apocalyptic view from the heights above the Manchegan plains recalls the subtitle of Alemán's novel, *Watchtower of Human Life*. The preachments contained in *Guzmán* make it all too clear that a baroque, theocentric faith in an authentic, better world after death sustains Alemán. Cela's *Lazarillo* unveils no such transcendental belief; rather, his protagonist is more to be associated with modern outcasts.

Lázaro finally arrives at one of the villages in La Mancha and spends a wretched night at an inn in a bed covered with a threadbare, vermin-filled mattress. Wry humor fills this account; the mean proprietress informs him that there is quite a varied menu, but after ordering a series of dishes, he learns that there is only dried beef. While in the village, he serves as

assistant to a stingy apothecary, Don Roque, who never pays
him. Lázaro is pleased to find a copy of the original *Lazarillo de
Tormes* because he supposes that it is about the adventures of
his grandfather. He says nothing to his master about having
found the book, not wanting the old man to know he has been
rummaging among the papers. One cannot ascertain how the
illiterate boy is able to read the novel since it is much later,
when he is in the army, that he is taught to read and write.
One would seem, then, to have here a slight lapse on Cela's
part.

Cela has referred to the finding of the original *Lazarillo* in
the druggist's shop in the opening lines of the *Nuevas andanzas*,
and now he says of its owner:

Don Roque was a descendant of Jews converted in the old days, and
some, among the more idle-tongued, insisted that he had a flute-like
voice, because he wasn't as he should be and the way all men are
. . . . (I, 479)

This remark and the fact that, after leaving the druggist, Lázaro
serves an old witch and fortune teller in the same town—not
moving on as was his habit—are preparations for the final effects
planned by the author.

The reference to Don Roque's Jewish ancestors needs to be
elaborated. Cela has been greatly influenced by those scholars
who insist on the all-pervasive effects that the symbiosis of
Semitic and Christian peoples has had on Spanish civilization,
ascribing to it a uniqueness that ignores the general Western
European heritage of the country. There are permanent re-
minders of the Moors in Spain. The importance of the Jews is
established by a study of Spanish history and literature, but the
fact that for centuries they no longer lived in the peninsula
makes them exotic, rather mysterious beings, so that even a
passing reference to a converted Jew is sure to intrigue most
Spanish readers.

At length, Cela builds up to an unusual, dramatic conclusion.
After a very harrowing night, Lázaro decides to flee, taking
refuge from the witch in some caves near the cemetery. Ap-

proaching footsteps reveal Don Roque, the homosexual pharmacist, meeting Luquitas, from a nearby town. "The Devil! The Devil!" resounds in Lázaro's ears as he runs for it across the fields (I, 508). In the Epilogue Lázaro reaches Madrid, is drafted into the army, and afterwards writes this account of his life, implying that he may write a sequel. In the Note of the Editor Cela affirms that he never found additional manuscript, but he hints at a second part. If the later books of vagabondage do not have ". . . the picaresque attitude, . . . the method is there: travel and instability."6 While they lack the picaro, they express the author's need to get out on the open road, away from society, to refresh his inspiration.

Although Cela does not succeed in adapting the genre to modern Spain, as did Mark Twain with *Huckleberry Finn* in the nineteenth-century United States, the reason does not lie entirely in lack of plot; the older picaresque novels did not have much intrigue or certain other novelistic elements in the present-day sense. The *Lazarillo* of Cela remains *sub specie aeternitatis,* and, charming as it may be, it is difficult for the modern reader to become emotionally or intellectually involved. Lázaro's induction into the army and a few references to hard times—a chronic condition in Spain in recent centuries—hardly make it a timely novel in the usual meaning.7

CHAPTER 5

Years of Transition

STUDIES of Cela's works have not considered the writings of the seven years between 1944 and 1951—the dates of the novels *Nuevas andanzas y desventuras de Lazarillo de Tormes* and *La colmena*—in relation to his developing novelistic style. During this period he published six volumes of sketches and short stories, the first of the books of vagabondage—*Viaje a la Alcarria*—and meanwhile continued to work on *La colmena*. An entire monograph could easily be devoted to the short stories, which are of value for showing the elaboration of his methods of observation and presentation which culminate in *La colmena*, but this brief chapter can include only a sampling.

I *The Young Storyteller*

Cela himself has told us how in 1941, almost by accident, he wrote his first short story. Friends on the journal *Medina* asked him to write a tale, and he replied: "Come, man, I don't know how to write stories, . . . if you want a poem . . . ."[1] Since then, the short fictional piece has become a regular part of his literary effort. In the prologue to the second volume of the *Obra completa*, the author does not distinguish clearly between the various genres; indeed, he claims to be unconcerned with the usual classifications, the main difference between the short story, the "apunte carpetovetónico," the short novel, and the novel being, in his opinion, merely one of weight by the scales (II, 21-22). It will be demonstrated, however, that with the publication of the third volume of sketches Cela attempts to separate and define the "apuntes" more clearly. There is substantial elaboration of technique between the first collection of short stories, *Esas nubes que pasan,* 1945, and *La colmena,* 1951. The title, *The Passing Clouds,* and the mood of the prefatory page—"The clouds over the city, lofty at times, like proud gentlemen in love; gray and taciturn, on occasion, like weary traveling beggars, like debtors who dislike the morning light" (II, 48) —remind one of the well-known "Las nubes" ("The Clouds") by Azorín. Cela's friends from an old seafaring town begin to appear so that, from the outset, the tone of the collection is colored by a melancholy reminiscence. Some of the stories are humorous, with occasional "tremendista" elements, grotesqueness, sentimentality, improbable coincidences and plots, and, at times, unlikely dialogue. Although the stories retain something of the conventionality of an earlier generation of Spanish writers, they nonetheless give evidence of his skill of treatment. Poetic and lyric flights are frequent and, by comparison, longer than those found in later writings.

The very first tale incorporates arbitrary, unconvincing, and only partially developed features, but has an amusing ending. Don Anselmo, whose name is the story's title, causes the proprietor of a shooting gallery to lose an eye accidentally, and friends advise that he go away for a few months even though the injury is not entirely his fault. Anselmo leaves behind a large sum to care for the poor man. After an absence of eight years, he returns with a Puerto Rican wife, two servants, and two parrots, all of whom die conveniently in one paragraph. Cela never hesitates to dispatch his characters—the *fatum* to which he alludes on occasion. To amuse himself, the lonely widower visits neighboring cities until one day he comes home in downcast mood. The victim of the shooting accident is now performing as a circus wild man, eating raw meat, and considers himself fortunate to have good pay and plenty to eat, but Don Anselmo is touched by such degradation.

Another composition, "El misterioso asesinato de la Rue Blanchard" ("The Mysterious Murder on Blanchard Street"), contains "tremendista" elements and a rather unlikely double "murder." One-legged Joaquín Bonhome attempts to give his repulsive wife a kick, with the result that a hook on the wall penetrates her glass eye and kills her; and he falls backward striking his head in such a way that he dies also. The wife's effete brother, whom the cripple has always despised, is sent to the French penal colony of Guiana for the supposed "crime."

"Don Juan," on the other hand, is a charming, deceptively simple account with the sentimental overtones of the traditional Spanish short story. A poet and amateur gardener, unable to find a publisher for his book on the care of flowers, dies, and when it no longer matters, one of his two surviving cronies pays for an edition of the work as a final tribute. Here the simplicity and naturalness of sentiments are an excellent combination. Other tales, however, are no more than anecdotes or jokes, for instance, "Don Homobono y los grillos" ("Mr. Goodfellow and the Crickets"). With a few platitudes about Mother Nature, the kindly protagonist saves a cricket from the clutches of a small boy, but later that hot August night when a cricket keeps him awake, the former benefactor swats the creature without compunction (II, 143-46). In the last story of the collection, "Culpemos a la primavera" ("Blame It on the Spring"), there is an amusing but overly ingenious plot involving the amorous intrigues of two servant girls, a milkmaid, a young brother and sister, the father of the family, and a neighboring doctor. To the mother's considerable vexation, a kind of spring madness affecting the characters leads to their love trysts. The story ends with four lines describing the mother's death and burial the following winter.

These rather ephemeral stories were first written for daily papers to amuse the casual reader who would hardly submit them to intense scrutiny. The humor of some is considerable and is much more gentle and humane than the sardonic irony of situations involving the apartment building of the homosexual in La colmena. It is well to remember that Cela has this light humorous vein; if one were to judge only on the basis of his two best-known novels, such talent would in all probability go unnoticed.

The contrast in range and variety of these scenes with the sustained hopelessness—or, at best, dreariness lightly touched by humor—of La colmena is striking. The episode of the im-

pecunious musician and the colored glasses, incorporated in
La colmena, was first published in *Arriba* (1946) as a short
story, and Cela includes it in volume II of the *Obra completa*
as the first of four "Cuentos al natural" ("Artless Stories")
which, except for their simplicity and a certain lack of anecdotal
quality in the usual sense, are not particularly homogeneous.
In "El capitán Jerónimo Expósito" (II, 231-35), the second of
the "Artless Stories," Captain Jerónimo, as the title implies, is
a foundling. The main idea seems to be that emerging from
nothing, he makes his own personality by organizing a band of
adventurers who, at the story's abrupt, rather pointless end,
await orders from their leader. Cela himself becomes aware of
the truncated outcome, and much later, in *Los viejos amigos*
(II, 65-67), adds three pages, continuing the story of the
group's departure from Algeciras for La Guayra. Nothing more
is ever heard from the men; so "they probably fell by the wayside." The narrator adds phlegmatically that if he ever learns
more about their exploits, he will not remain silent. Although
most of the persons in *La colmena* lead aimless lives, curiously
the writing about them is charged with implications. The "Captain Jerónimo" as it stands lacks the incidental or circumstantial
elements necessary to a story; it reads like a note for a longer
account of a minor epic of crime, high adventure, or just plain
frustration. The last selection of this series has the general
heading "Fauna del adoquinado" ("Fauna of the Pavement")
and the subtitle "El prodigio de que un niño viva como un
saltamontes" ("The Miracle that a Child Can Live like a
Grasshopper"), II, 241-43. The boy reminds one vaguely of
the little gypsy street dancer in *La colmena,* but at the story's
end we are told that the lad may grow up to be a taxi driver,
notary, carpenter, or priest so that he is pretty much like many
others of his age. There is a note of wistfulness for the carefree
days of youth which most men, in common with the author,
feel at times.

Cela's short stories range from the brutal—at least two contain crimes as violent and senseless as those in *Pascual Duarte*
—to the purely humorous, lyric, ironic, commonplace, burlesque,
or caricatural. One describes a young writer, C.J.C., on a train

composing an insipid story "in the old style" (II, 207-11); some
are about everyday situations, but with a certain imaginary
dimension or even fantasy; and still others are about Galicia
and include songs in the local dialect of that region. The inspiration for "La horca" ("The Gibbet") came to Cela after
listening to Ravel's music at a friend's house (II, 452-56). A
section on watches and clocks provides the pretext for narratives like that of the gypsy who has a cracker tin filled with
stolen timepieces until the police of the Guardia Civil arrest
him and confiscate it. The gypsy is partly consoled when a
fellow prisoner gives him a watch; it is still in his possession
many years later when he dies (II, 351-61). In these stories
Cela demonstrates the inventiveness that writers for the popular press often have—the ability to take almost any object as
a suggestion from which to spin a yarn—but his is a far superior
style. At times there is a frankly sentimental note, as in the tales
about a blind man's dog and a sea-going dog (II, 523-29), or
allegory as in the fables anthropomorphizing the outlaw goat
named Smith (II, 316-25) and the migration of the body lice
in "La tierra de promisión" ("The Promised Land"), II, 212-15.
"Claudius, profesor de idiomas" ("Claudius, Professor of Languages"), II, 184-98, is possibly one of his best stories: its
plot is based on the series of chance meetings, typical of two
acquaintances who see each other infrequently. The friend is
identified briefly as the former hangman of Batavia in the
Dutch East Indies, who now bustles around from one edifying
cultural activity to another. At length, he remarks, "I am wor-
ried, my friend; in Batavia I must be so far behind in my work!"
Either death has taken a holiday, or Claudius, like Camus' Sisyphus, is unable, or really does not want, to escape his absurd
vocation.

This sampling of themes from Cela's short stories shows his
innate talent for creating literature from all manner of materials,
an ability sometimes displayed in feats of virtuosity. The important thing to bear in mind is that his latent capacity to
chronicle the everyday, vulgar existence of ordinary people is
brought forth by a closer observation of his surroundings, first,
in rural settings and then in Madrid, where he comes to grips

with the harsh realities of urban life after the ruinous Civil War. Had Cela continued in the earlier vein, he might be remembered as a clever storyteller of modest talent. He needed to escape from the world of literature and contemplate people as they live in order to add sinew to a facile style.

II *The Grass Roots*

Viaje a la Alcarria will be discussed in a later chapter, together with other works of the same type. For the moment it is necessary to mention that Cela presents his observations of half-forgotten towns in a region close to Madrid where, as he says, he saw no unusual happenings and was glad, because if it were necessary to narrate out-of-the-ordinary events, people would accuse him of exaggerating (IV, 28). So, the various short stories included in *El gallego y su cuadrilla y otros apuntes carpetovetónicos* (1949) offer the humdrum, everyday life of small towns. The almost untranslatable term "carpetovetónico" has come to refer to "the dryness, the violent, bitter spirit of contrast and rudeness of the world of sun-scorched and dusty Castile."[2] The word itself derives from the names of two central Iberian tribes mentioned by Roman writers. The towns are little places through which the traveler today drives without even a fleeting thought as to their inhabitants, but where life goes on beneath an exterior as unchanging as the harsh land. Critics have been quick to point out parallels between his "apuntes" and the sketches of customs and regions of nineteenth-century writers.[3] But there is a great difference in spirit and locale between the works of such authors and those of Cela, who has deliberately avoided the picturesqueness of a Pereda, for example. He neither visits old churches searching for almost forgotten artistic treasures, nor is he a landscapist. He turns to the little-known, unexplored towns of the Old Castile so fascinating to writers of the Generation of 1898—none of those cited by Cela are natives of the province—and finds that "Castile is at first a bit like a narcotic of bitter and hard draughts which does not affect the Castilian who is already an addict, but which startles and frightens the stranger" (V, 137).

Other regions attract tourists and vacationers because of
benign climate, local color, cultural importance, mountain and
seaside resorts, or other pleasant settings. Rodríguez-Moñino
puts it well in his prologue to Cela's *El gallego y su cuadrilla*
when he declares that city dwellers of Madrid, Barcelona, and
Bilbao do not spend holidays in places like Cebreros, where
Cela during four summers returned for lengthy visits.[4]

The weariness which small towns produce in us, the dry Castilian
and Estremaduran towns, comes from a feeling expressed concretely
in these words: they do not have any personality, they are all alike,
nothing ever happens in them, they are boring and monotonous.

If one must spend a few days in such places, he at first feels
out of his element, then antipathy, and finally frank aversion.
And Rodríguez-Moñino asks: "What did Cela do in that place
where there is nothing to do? He lived. Lived and saw how one
lives." Like a taproot the author was able to extract from beneath an inhospitable surface the moisture sufficient to nourish
a luxuriant growth, so that ". . . he has penetrated deeply the
life and essence of those places and has been pouring out in
the pages of this book the fruits of a really amazing psychological observation."

Cela has defined the "apunte carpetovetónico" as something
invented for his exclusive use, ". . . that little, startled chronicle
of the dry lands of Spain, that inexhaustible vein of literary
themes" (III, 23). The "notes"—"jottings" would be applicable
on occasion—may be as rigid as sticks, but articulation is not
necessary to show "this, that, or something else. Unlike the
article, the 'apunte' is neither born nor dies, but simply flows
out and disappears. . . . it may well have neither beginning
nor end . . ." (III, 787-88). And it is not a short story which
at times expresses an abstraction or permits subjectivism; the
objectivity of the "apunte" is fundamental. The author places
himself before the commonplace locales with no special artistic
or emotional attitude toward them, but, of course, must select
material and clothe it in literary language. This will be his
same approach in *La colmena*. Small details permit a display

of his skill with words, as in the long paragraph on the flies of Cebreros—quite likely a reflection of "Las moscas" ("The Flies") of Antonio Machado, a poet whom Cela greatly admires. Attention to small creatures or objects is a characteristic of the Generation of 1898. Whatever the traditional affinities of these sketches, there is no denying that Cela caused the attention of his contemporaries to turn once more to local settings for inspiration. One of the best, Miguel Delibes' appealing novel *Las ratas (The Rats)*, has as its locale a tiny hamlet near Valladolid in Old Castile.

An essential of Cela's technique is the ability to suggest in a few details or mannerisms an entire character or situation. He locates precisely the boundaries of Cebreros, but captures its essential Castilian isolation thus:

The town is far from the railroad, far from the main highway, far from the river, hidden in the shadow of the parish church tower, an Herreran tower of old granite which the drought of four centuries, that drought which denuded Castile, has not allowed to grow the affectionate, silent, greenish moss of age. (III, 48)

In his *Lazarillo* Cela speaks feelingly of the village idiot, also the subject of one of the best sketches in *El gallego*. With humor and sympathy he endows this much abused type with the dignity afforded the average villager. The town will not support more than one such moron at a time; so Blas Herrero Martínez —he is honored with a full set of names—has to wait until the ancient Perejilondo dies before taking over the position. Meanwhile, on Sunday Blas serves his apprenticeship by gathering cigarette butts in Doña Luisita's café for the old "tonto," who gives him a half-dozen as his pay. Finally the old man dies, and the young Blas secretly dances for joy; then realizing that he must show some signs of grief, he makes a point of visiting the grave of the deceased where he leaves all but his usual six butts. Gradually he forgets about his dead predecessor and collects only as many as he wants: "It was a strange sensation to squat down and pick up a butt and have no doubt that it was one's very own . . ." (III, 119). The village idiot is a

familiar type the world over, as anyone who has ever lived in a
small town may know; but seldom has the absurdity of every
man's role in this world been so aptly expressed.

In an effort to show the new direction Cela's writing will
take, only a few of the best sketches will be discussed. In "El
café de la Luisita" ("Luisita's Café"), III, 124-26, he dedicates
paragraphs to each café in Cebreros with such skillful choice
of details that one can visualize the coffeehouses and the particular clientele they attract. Luisita's café is given a more precise description, including a summary presentation of the
proprietress and her husband: "Luisita, who was over fifty
years of age, was fat and always on duty. Her husband was a
scrawny, faded drunk, no longer good for anything" (III, 125).
In the last paragraph the writer mentions the bars and taverns
of the town and the human fauna which frequents them, but
"to talk about all those taverns and their inhabitants would
take a whole volume." In *La colmena* Cela does indeed give us
a novel populated largely by habitués of cafés and bars.

"Doña Concha" portrays the incredibly monotonous life of
a childless lady in a small town and her secret envy of the
married sister with ten children, to whom she has willed her
property. ". . . The nephews don't know this and they do not
wish her dead. Doña Concha hardly knows her nephews . . ."
(III, 91).

"Toros en Cebreros" ("Bullfight in Cebreros") is almost an
editorial in favor of preserving the old custom of the local
bullfight that a shortage of funds threatens with suspension.
Cela points out that the Spaniard is more likely to revolt because some hallowed custom is threatened than because he is
hungry, that historically the people usually had a reason for
rebellion although their excesses might cause them to lose sight
of it in twenty-four hours. In *Arriba,* where this and many other
early sketches were first published, the censorship cut out
three rather innocuous paragraphs of ironical references to
local administrators (III, 61-63). "El gallego y su cuadrilla,"
bearing the title of the collection, describes a small-town bullfight in the province of Toledo (III, 130-35). Here, on a blister-
ingly hot, dusty day, there is no glamor of the great bullrings:

the "toreros" fight in shirt sleeves, not in the "suit of lights";
there is no band; and the arena is the town square, closed off by
wagons and barricades. In a sequel, "Baile en la plaza" ("Dance
in the Square"), bloody streams from the slain bull and the
fatally injured matador mingle in the plaza, and the peasants
are careful to wet the soles of their hempen sandals in the gore
so as to make them hard and to insure longer wear. The author
shifts back and forth from the dying bullfighter to the flirting
couple dancing in the square (III, 136-39), thus employing
a technique that he will use with proficiency in *La colmena*.

"Una función de varietés" ("A Vaudeville Performance") is
broadly humorous. Cela interrupts his narration of the banal
performance to describe the Ballet Hollywood's great success
with the town's womanizers, who later invite the girls of the
troupe to a party in the anisette factory. Their womenfolk inter-
rupt the gathering and exchange unflattering remarks with the
girls. After this digression, the amusing account of the program
and the grand finale continues, and finally: "The curtain rose
and fell many times and the people began to file out. The
vaudeville had ended. A little later was when the episode of
the anisette factory transpired" (III, 146-49).

In the excellent "La romería" ("The Pilgrimage"), III, 93-111,
there is a wealth of everyday experience in the account of a typical family outing—a hike—with the customary physical dis-
comforts and minor personality conflicts of a hot, thirsty, boring
day with the usual wasp sting, sunburn, and other irritations.
On the return trip the family ". . . found itself near the first
lights of the town. A sigh of relief, very low, was audible within
each breast" (III, 109). The mother-in-law, characteristically,
has the last word to which the dispirited daughter and husband
do not even bother to reply.

These sketches have little relation with short stories built
around dramatic or picturesque incidents, much less with those
where there is emphasis on plot development. Here Cela's
ability to turn a phrase to point up the utter triviality, monotony,
or commonplaceness of life or, for that matter, death in a small
Spanish town has become a fundamental process with him.
Even where a topic might be elaborated with colorful or emo-

tional language, he tends to understatement and restraint, with few false notes—an important development in the transition from his earlier "tremendista" tendencies.

Cela's ability to capture essential personality with a gesture, mannerism, or other trait recalls to some critics the neo-realistic or behaviorist approach of those who believe that traditional novels, attempting to portray internal psychology, lack validity and concentrate on externals with almost photographic objectivity; but these outward manifestations are only significant if equated with something fundamental in the subject's temperament.[5] Cela repeats the outward peculiarities of his characters to facilitate rapid identification.

CHAPTER 6

The Big City

C ELA'S increased power as a portrayer of Spanish life is
the result of faithful observation and constant writing
during the periods of his lengthy visits to Cebreros. He gained
a deeper insight into the mentality of the Spanish people, the
basic theme of his most significant work. In this rural microcosm,
isolated from the distractions of the city, he was able to develop
an instinct for capturing the essentials of individuals and scenes
in a few descriptive lines. *La colmena,* still considered Cela's
masterpiece by many, evolved in the years from 1945 to 1950,
and one of its vignettes was published separately in 1946. It is
important to bear in mind his developing technique of this
period because critics have seriously proposed Dos Passos' *Manhattan Transfer* as his model for the presentation of urban life
in a series of loosely connected sketches.[1] This American novel
had been translated in Spain before the war, but as the preceding chapter shows, Cela has been steadily elaborating his own
method. The action of *La colmena* is concentrated, whereas that
of Dos Passos' rambling novel covers twenty years and the sections are much longer. Evidently, *Manhattan Transfer* is cited
in an effort to explain the great evolution in Cela's writing after
Pascual Duarte.[2]

In *La colmena* Cela for the first time deals at length and effectively with everyday urban life, thereby assuring his status as
Spain's foremost novelist. He surpasses the limitations of rural,
regionalistic literature with its inevitable ties to the presentation
of provincial customs—a traditional, fecund aspect of Spanish
literature still possessing considerable vitality in a country of so

many contrasts. According to Cela, *La colmena* presents the
petty lives and miseries of some 160 characters; in a note to
the first edition, the publisher states that there are 296 imaginary
characters and fifty names of real persons, a total of 346.[3] The
most useful way of putting it, perhaps, is to say that there are
some forty-eight principals who appear and reappear in the
novel.[4]

I *The Teeming Hive*

In the "Nota" to the first edition of *La colmena* (Buenos Aires,
1951), Cela comments that its structure ". . . is complex and has
cost me a lot of work. . . . The 160 persons who bustle, they do
not run, through its pages have led me for five long years down
a bitter path." Certainly his work does not aim to be anything
more ". . . than a slice of life narrated step by step, without
vacillation, without strange tragedies, without charity, just as
life passes. Whether we like it or not."

No Spanish publisher would touch the novel. Cela has recently
discussed the literary climate of this period in Spain. After the
innovation of "tremendismo" and the appearance of *La colmena*,
Spanish writing takes a "new direction . . . along the path . . .
of objective narration, which in its . . . maturity gave rise to
a new flowering of the so-called social literature, old as the
world itself." That this path has been followed by very few
writers is due to Spain's isolation from the rest of the world;
Cela insists that "literature . . . is a tradition which breaks
down when it is channeled or dammed up in the service of a
political creed" (*PSA*, no. LXXIX [1962], 15-16). He places emphasis upon the modern writer's attempt to maintain his integrity—a subject that has become a preoccupation with him.
Perhaps one of the most encouraging spiritual manifestations in
countries whose governments regiment the arts into officially
approved channels is the predictable tendency of some writers
to seek a free portrayal of conditions as they see them. In spite
of harassment, the activities of certain Russian authors in the
past decade are heartening, not because they necessarily imply
a defeat of communism, but because on a larger scale they re-

store a faith in humanism and freedom of conscience for which contemporary society has supplied no substitute.

While Cela's pitiless description of Spanish life does not directly criticize the present regime, and his implied dissatisfaction may seem mild to readers in countries where vociferous political opposition is the rule, it should be remembered that even "disrespect" for governmental institutions may lead to severe punishment under a dictatorship. An article in the *New York Times,* February 17, 1967, p. 12, reports that the Justice Commission of the Spanish Parliament approved an addition to the Penal Code providing penalties even for ". . . persons who fail to show 'due respect' to institutions and officials by criticizing the political or administrative acts of the institutions and officials." This act is aimed particularly at writers, editors, and publishers ". . . disseminating 'false or dangerous' information on subjects ranging from *public morals* [italics mine] to state security and national defense." Already in January, 1967, the writer Miguel Sánchez Mazas Ferlosio, charged with insults to the Chief of State and illegal propaganda, had been sentenced to twelve years in prison "for rebellion."

La colmena is really the subtitle of a proposed series called *Los caminos inciertos (Uncertain Roads),* of which no further works have yet been published, a title suggestive of Sartre's *Les Chemins de la liberté.*[5] The resemblance, however, may be purely fortuitous since the content in some ways recalls Baroja's trilogy *La lucha por la vida (The Struggle for Life),* with its concern for social problems. Cela's novel is short, 257 pages in the English edition,[6] and covers a period of some three days in December, 1943, datable from a tombstone toward the end (253) and a reference to the meeting of Churchill, Stalin, and Roosevelt at Teheran in November, 1943 (233). Spain in the bitter aftermath of the Civil War is thus seen against the larger conflict of World War II, and brief references throughout the novel to the course of the war remind the reader of the worldwide struggle. The possibility that the Axis powers might not win may have caused Cela and other Spaniards to reconsider their own situation.

Ilie gives a succinct analysis of the element of time in *La colmena*.[7] The action covers a period from the afternoon of the first day to the night of the second, with an epilogue taking place one morning four or five days later. The first and second chapters are in chronological order—the afternoon and early evening of the first day. The third chapter interrupts the sequence to jump to the afternoon of the second day, to be interrupted in turn by the fourth which returns to the night of the first day. The fifth chapter jumps forward to the night of the second, while the sixth returns to the morning of that same day. By breaking up the movement of time in this manner, the author gives an impression of continual present. Cela is successful with this technique because the individual stories are not complex, and in hopping from one to the other there is no problem in picking up the simple thread of the narrative. The cutting up of the action and splicing in a non-chronological sequence produces a cinematic effect. Even though it is useful that the reader bear in mind this order of events, it is not a procedure that will cause confusion. Cela does not go to the extremes of Juan Rulfo, the Mexican novelist, who in *Pedro Páramo* (1955) has been accused of cutting his manuscript into fragments and arbitrarily pasting them back together.[8] Cela's illogical time sequence may at first irritate the reader used to normal chronology, but the treatment has been so skillful that the novel has a logic of its own. In a longer work such a technique could become unmanageable and may provide one explanation for Cela's failure to continue the proposed trilogy—although in a recent letter he declares that he never seriously considered doing so. Much depends upon the author's genius for furnishing, sometimes in half a page or less, the essentials of a particular character so that whenever or wherever he is met again identification will be easy. It has been said that for minor characters all Cela provides is a single gesture,[9] but with it he captures the essential attribute, just as surely as does the painter Zuloaga when he sketches the portrait of an Andalusian bullfighter after seeing nothing more than the manner in which the "torero" adjusts the "montera" on his head before entering the ring. Special attention to basic details is all the more necessary because there is a certain sameness of tone to the lives of so many of the people in *La colmena*. In spite of their poverty and degradation, they strive to maintain a vestige of self-respect.[10] Their effort, in an environment threatening at any moment to annihilate them, preserves their identity, whether one wishes to regard it as an existential struggle or as a timeless contest against evil—an evil here considered as the epitome of all that is negative in the world. So, after a page-long description of the brutalities of her past life, what lies at the bottom of the rather jaded Elvira's behavior is summed up in a few lines: "The poor girl is somewhat embittered, but not overmuch. She has good instincts and, timid though she is, a remnant of pride" (25). The prostitute has broken with Don Pablo and is loath to resume relations, even though to do so would improve her distressing financial situation.

To other characters as well, pride gives a sense of identification, hollow or unauthentic as it may be in an existentialist context. Speaking to the bootblack in the café, Don Leonardo Meléndez opens with his favorite phrase: "We, the Meléndez, an age-old line connected with the most ancient families of Castile, were once upon a time the masters of lands and lives. Today . . . we're practically in the middle of *la rue*" (23). Earlier, Don Leonardo has bilked the bootblack out of his life savings of 30,000 pesetas (4), and still the victim is flattered that such a distinguished man deigns to speak, even curtly, to him. Señor Suárez, the homosexual, appears to be, and may very well be, a prosperous businessman; after a silly telephone conversation in the café with his boyfriend, he makes his grand exit, "holding his head high like a Roman gladiator, oozing satisfaction, radiating bliss" (20). Later he will be seen in the most ridiculous situations and will be the subject of the most unflattering remarks.

Cela prefaces the 1965 edition of his novelette *Café de artistas* by quoting Santiago Ramón y Cajal: "When I am in the café, I feel more Spanish than ever" (III, 621). And, indeed, it is not surprising that much of the action in *La colmena*, if such a term really applies, revolves around the café of Doña Rosa. The afternoon and evening gatherings ("tertulias") of friends, in groups related to their interests—social pursuits, bullfighting, literature, business, or guitar playing—have long been an important feature of Spanish life. The custom still exists, but some of the old cafés are disappearing; it is depressing to learn that one of the best known, frequented by journalists, has been replaced by a chic sporting-goods shop. It is said that the model for Doña Rosa's place in the Glorieta de Bilbao has been taken over by a bank.

In *La colmena*, nevertheless, there is little of the usual camaraderie of the "tertulia." On rare occasions one encounters a group of people gathered to play dominoes or talk. Rather, the author takes us from one person or couple to another without transitional remarks, with the apparent objectivity of the camera lens, and later with the same technique focuses on them at home, in a restaurant, in a brothel, or on the street. There is not, then, a single protagonist or even a group drawn together for the author's purpose. Since he believes that ". . . from each life there are born half a dozen different lives" (II, 168), he is able to use the common denominator of Doña Rosa's café for a successful integration of all types in the novel. If some do not appear in the café, others who are to serve as links between them do. Thus, the homosexual, although not a regular patron of the café, is introduced to us there so that the later murder of his mother and the resultant clustering of people in the apartment building will permit the presentation of quite a variety of additional characters. Just before our first meeting with Señor Suárez, Cela introduces a "new customer" of the café who chats with the cigarette boy: "His name is Mauricio Segovia and he works at the Central Telephone Exchange. I mention all this because he may turn up again" (19). And indeed he does, several times—the last occasion being when he is out for a night on the town with his brother and they wind up at the same bar where the homosexual Suárez is having a tryst with his friend Pepe the Chip.

Of this novelistic procedure Cela himself has remarked that "*La colmena* is a novel like a watch, . . . made up of little parts which are all necessary, each for the other, so that the whole thing can run." [11] He often cites Dostoevski, and while a search does not disclose the famous quotation, "Each man is responsible to everyone for everything," anywhere in his works, the words of Dostoevski are an apt description of the human inter-relationships in *La colmena*. Some critics[12] have missed in this novel of the multiple protagonist the lengthy character portrayal of the traditional novel; or it is felt that Cela should at least have provided characters of greater depth, like those of Aldous Huxley's *Point Counter Point*,[13] and he is even blamed for the abortive efforts of his imitators. It is evident that both critics and unsuccessful followers of his method have missed somehow an important facet of the book: Cela is not trying for psychological depth, personality change, or denouement resulting from anagnorisis in the usual sense, as was suggested at the end of the preceding chapter. Some readers do not particularly care for short stories partly because formal requirements often result not only in skimpy characterization, but, worse, in inconsistencies or loose ends that cannot be concealed in a short space. No doubt in the longer novel, discrepancies are also present, but the mass of story material effectively hides them. If one were to assemble into a single account all the passages in *La colmena* where a more important personage appears, it would be rare to find such defects. By fragmenting a single story into a mosaic of relationships with others, who in turn are connected with still others in the narration, there is not only a sort of mathematical progression which effectively creates the impression of the multifarious connections—at times intimate, at times casual—of a whole society, but the individual, although in one sense an anonymous hero, paradoxically stands out in sharper relief.

This last effect is obtained by eliminating much of the description of externals—settings and transitional passages—so common to most novels. There are some four dozen significant persons in the book, presented for the first time briefly but carefully, so that without preliminary words the reader can identify them later in another scene or action. This economy of narration not only permits the author to pack into his novel the number of characters that would normally fill a much larger volume, but, strangely enough, this procedure secures the co-operation of the reader in a satisfactory manner. If one's recol-

lection of a certain individual is hazy, it is probably no more
so than in the traditional novel where the plethora of other
characters and descriptive detail obscures any one individual.
The fact that Cela's method facilitates rapid reading aids the
process of apprehension. It would be inaccurate to say that at
a first perusal there are no moments when the reader cannot
quite place a person he has met only once before, but the impression of immediacy makes the action of the moment similar
to real-life encounters with acquaintances in public places so
that any memory lapse is unimportant. The work is a careful
assembling of bits and pieces that receives part of its unity
from the detailed and sympathetic portrayal of such people as
Martín Marco or the young poet Ramón Malleo among the
various patrons of Doña Rosa's café at the beginning. Ramón's
straitened circumstances and bad health—he collapses and slides
under a table and is taken into the men's room to recuperate—
are presented with obvious feeling by the author, who doubtless is recounting similar experiences of his early days as a writer.
Martín hopes to obtain a job in one of the syndicate, or union,
offices where, if the heating is good (255), he can do some
writing; it was under such circumstances that Cela wrote *La
familia de Pascual Duarte*.

II *A Modern Mosaic*

By tracing the movements of Martín Marco, one can outline
the basic structure of *La colmena*. Doña Rosa orders him ejected
from the café because he cannot pay for his coffee, and tells the
waiter to kick him a few times, but the kindly Galician refrains.
Martín, going off down the street, "looks at the city with the
eyes of a sick and harassed child" (50-51). As he passes a plumb-
ing store and idly looks at the fixtures, he thinks of toilet tanks
where a few books might be kept—Hölderlin, Keats, Valéry for
constipation; Rubén Darío, Mallarmé, ". . . especially Mallarmé,
for diarrhea . . ." (55). After a subway ride he arrives at his
married sister's house; he detests the husband, but the sister
takes care of him and provides him a bite to eat when she can
spare it (62-64). Martín next appears at Celestino's bar, the

Aurora—Celestino is a reader of Nietzsche's *Aurora* and dreams of heroic deeds quite contrary to his real nature. The café proprietor hesitates to serve him more coffee since his overdue bill is already quite high, and Martín, in a dudgeon, calls him a pharisee and petty bourgeois, leaves in a huff, and has a brief encounter on the street with his friend Paco, who wonders why he did not wait in the bar for him.

The well-to-do friend Pablo Alonso allows Martín to spend the nights in a storeroom at his home; some space in the book is devoted to Pablo's love affair with his mistress Laurita (59-61, 70-72, 99-100). Martín spends his mornings at the Central Post Office or Bank of Spain writing poetry on the backs of telegraph forms or deposit slips. We then see him at a café with his friend Ventura Aguado (105-6). In the course of their conversation he refers to his girlfriend Purita, a prostitute, and, characteristically for Cela's technique in this novel, the scene shifts to this girl out on a date with a rich junk dealer.

The appearance of Ventura Aguado brings in other threads of the story. Ventura is having an affair with Julita, daughter of Doña Visi and Don Roque (119-21). Doña Visi is also the sister of Doña Rosa, the proprietress of the café featured so prominently at the beginning of the novel. Other elements of the story revolve around Julita's parents. There is the ridiculously devout friend of the mother, Doña Monserrat, enthusiastic about the conversion of Chinese children and a reader of the *Missionary Cherub* (108-13, 133-34). She is truly vexed at a blasphemous parrot, Rabelais, on the third floor of the building and wants to report it to the police, quite likely a dig at the practice common in police states of denouncing wrongdoers on a mere whim. The father tells the woman not to be silly. Don Roque himself is carrying on with Lola, the younger sister of a former maid with whom he has also been intimate (109). Lola is much more promiscuous and has been friendly with Ventura, the lover of Roque's daughter. The situation comes to a head when Don Roque goes to Doña Celia's house of assignation and meets his own daughter on the stairs as she is leaving from a tryst with Ventura (216-20). Cela changes time sequences so quickly that one can be misled as to the chronol-

ogy of events. At the end of the account of Don Roque's meeting with Lola, the reader is informed that Lola was particularly upset because her distracted lover has no desire for her
after the meeting on the stairs with his daughter. For revenge
she takes down a photo of Doña Celia's deceased husband and
mails it to Julita, who of course recognizes it since she and
Ventura have shared the same room. Julita shows the photo
to Ventura and he sends it with a cryptic threatening note to
Don Roque (196-97), who thinks it is the work of Freemasons.
However, the business of the photo is a mystery until Lola's
action and motives are explained nearly twenty-five pages later.

This digression from the account of Martín's activities is
presented to show the ramifications in the development of the
story as one traces the relationships between the characters
from one to another. Minor details are also important to the
structure of the novel. So, when Martín is with Ventura Aguado,
the friend lends him twenty-five pesetas. Martín generously pays
for the two coffees and is left with twenty-two pesetas (106),
the exact sum that he owes to the bar owner, Celestino. In the
brief section immediately preceding, Petrita, the maid of Martín's sister, feels such great sympathy for the young man that
she gives herself to Celestino to cancel the debt. The fact that
these small sums of money assume great importance underscores
the penury of many of the characters.

Martín continues his peregrinations through Madrid. After
some twenty pages we see him chatting on the street with a
friend from his student days, Nati Robles, a rather over-dressed,
prosperous, but lonesome girl. The two go off to a café to talk
about old times (127-29), and there he cadges fifty pesetas from
her; after he pays for the drinks, she suggests that he buy her
a present with the change. There follows a flashback to the
night of the preceding day when Celestino fumes at Martín's
arrogance about the debt of twenty-two pesetas, and Martín is
shown chatting with an Argentine prostitute called the "Uru-
guayan" and sponging coffee, brandy, and a cigar off her date.
Petrita, the servant girl who secretly loves Martín, meanwhile
is having a rendezvous with the Galician policeman, Julio García
Morrazo, one of the habitués of Celestino's bar. Their meeting

takes place on the cold ground near the bullring (170-71).

With some logic, therefore, the scene shifts immediately to Martín still wandering the city streets, reluctant to go to bed, and the time of the novel has shifted back to the night of the first day, when Martín does not have a cent. He sits on a bench in the Plaza de Salamanca and smokes a cigarette stub from a collection he keeps in an envelope labeled "City Council of Madrid, Identity Cards Department" (172-73). Later on he will get into trouble because he has no identity papers. Seeking a little warmth, he makes the rounds of the houses of assignation, reflecting that the maid Petrita is a good girl and the longer she preserves her chastity the better; sooner or later some fishmonger or policeman will tumble her. A policeman with a gold tooth stops and searches him. He stammers that he left his papers at home, and to his great relief the policeman lets him go. "There is a terrible fear in his very bones, a fear that is past understanding" (175-78).

Delirious from dread and illness, Martín, gibbering about the gold tooth—that modest symbol of affluence and power—rushes on until exhausted (179-81); he finds refuge for the night in Doña Jesusa's brothel. She is sympathetic to Martín, who ". . . is not amused by kindness. Fundamentally, Martín, too, is a follower of Nietzsche." These scattered allusions to the German philosopher show that Cela still retained something of a youthful fascination for this thought as he understood it. Doña Jesusa sends Martín to bed with one of the girls, ironically named Pura, who is not feeling well. "Where tenderness is absent you try to find warmth. Pura and Martín throw all their clothing on the bed to be warmer, . . . and go to sleep in one another's arms like two newlyweds" (185-87). The fourth chapter ends with one of the few direct statements by the author: "And several dozens of girls are hoping—what are they hoping for, O God? Why do You let them be thus deceived?—with their minds full of golden dreams? . . . "

Chapter Five jumps to the night of the second day. Martín returns to Doña Rosa's café, where he was thrown out the day before for not paying. With the money from Nati in his pocket, he loftily orders coffee, pays off his debt, and calls for the bootblack. Before leaving the café, he goes to the lavatory, and when he takes out his handkerchief, a twenty-five peseta note slips unnoticed to the floor (214-15). His loss has important consequences for the impoverished musician Seoane, who, a few pages later, goes to the washroom and finds the money; his difficulty over how to provide dark glasses for his wife's eye trouble is now resolved (218-19). Dark glasses of decent quality sell at ridiculously high prices in Spain; such things are not for the average person. Although it is late, Martín goes to a friend's shop to buy the present for Nati; he selects a nice print of Venus, but when he reaches for the money, he discovers that the twenty-five pesetas are missing (227-30).

Chapter Six, a quite brief one, takes place the morning of this same day. Martín is still in bed with Pura at Doña Jesusa's. They listen to the cleaning women, washerwomen, and ironers at their work. Cela recounts in detail the lives of several, some of whom, although not all, have been prostitutes (233-39). Pura has five pesetas and orders breakfast for herself and Martín (241-42). Three short paragraphs conclude the chapter: one describes the murdered mother of the homosexual Suárez on the slab at the morgue, another shows the aging tart Elvira in her bed, and the third describes with a mixture of lyricism and despair the coming of morning to the teeming city where existence is likened to the struggle to climb a greased pole.

The morning unfolds slowly; it creeps like a caterpillar over the hearts of men and women in the city; it beats, almost caressingly, against the newly wakened eyes, eyes which never once discover new horizons, new landscapes, new settings.

And yet, this morning, this eternally repeated morning, has its little game changing the face of the city, of that tomb, that greased pole, that hive . . .

May God have mercy on us all. (242-43)

The "Finale" (244-57), occurring three or four days later, is really concerned with Martín, although he is generally referred to obliquely. Friends learn from reading the section of official notices and edicts in the newspaper that he is wanted by the police because his papers are not in order. The sister and

brother-in-law are concerned, but do not know what to do.
Pablo Alonso is in bed with his mistress Laurita. Martín has
already left Pablo's house to go to the cemetery to visit his
mother's grave on the anniversary of her death. Pablo does not
know this fact and decides to look for his friend in the usual
morning haunts, the Central Post Office or the Bank of Spain.
Paco and Celestino talk in the bar and decide that the best
thing to do is send Martín off to Barcelona before the police
get him. Doña Jesusa reads a few lines from the newspaper to
Purita, whom she meets on the Calle de Torrijos, and predicts
that nothing good will happen to the boy now. Ventura Aguado
calls Julita and sends her off to inform Martín's sister, while
he goes to make contact with an influential friend. Martín's
brother-in-law talks by phone to his boss, Señor Ramón, to
explain his absence from the office, and the boss agrees to hide
Martín for a few days if necessary. Meanwhile Martín has
passed through the miserable hovels on the outskirts of the city
and reached the cemetery. Rómulo, in his shop, reads the notice
in the newspaper and remarks, "That's the last drop. Some fel-
lows are Jonahs" (252). The inscription on the mother's grave
informs us that she died nine years before, December 20, 1934;
thus indirectly a definite date is provided for the end of the
novel. Martín, attempting to pray, cannot even remember "The
Lord's Prayer" correctly. His sister is in tears at home. The
brother-in-law and his employer have decided that the best
thing the young man can do is report to the police at once;
Captain Ovejero, or Don Tesifonte as he is most often called,
a member of Señor Ramón's group of friends who gather in
the café every afternoon to play dominoes (95), will be asked
to serve as his guarantee. Celestino has written three letters and
plans to write three more; he is preoccupied with Martín's problem and will not leave him in the lurch even though Martín
does not pay him. The object of all this furious activity is
supremely unaware of what is going on; he gets a paper from
the cemetery attendant and, not seeing the notice about himself, heads back to the city.

Since this novel does not have the conventional story line,
Cela is not concerned with Martín's eventual fate; neither has

he developed the theme of the murder of the homosexual's
mother. The elaboration of either topic is suitable for a novel
of intrigue or mystery, but, here, Cela is primarily interested in
presenting the various facets of Madrid life by emphasizing
the immediate situations of the people involved. The reader is
undoubtedly curious about the possible outcome of these di-
lemmas, but the deliberate fragmentation of events prevents a
deep involvement or identification with any one individual.
For this reason, perhaps, some critics have felt that all the
characters of La colmena are underdeveloped. The detailed account of Martín's activities proves that such is not the case, but
even his characterization is so interwoven with an equally vigorous presentation of the lives of others that he does not become
a protagonist. At the time Cela possibly planned to continue
with Martín in volume two of the proposed trilogy so that a
tidying of loose ends would now hardly be necessary. Simply
because Martín is thinking vaguely of getting a job, one should
not see a note of optimism in the ending of the novel; nor is
such a hopeful view of the circumstances necessary.[14]

III *Money and Sex*

It has been said that money and sex are the two main themes
of La colmena.[15] There is a close relationship between the two,
but behind both is the even greater plight of the misery of
hunger, cold, and sickness. The basic human need to satisfy
hunger and alleviate misery arouses a feeling of compassion for,
or at least an understanding of, the activities of the characters
in this novel. To the prosperous and well-fed, these people lead
sordid lives. Indeed they do. Yet if one recalls the devastated
cities of Europe in the wake of the advancing Allied armies of
World War II—the families broken up by the holocaust, the
fatalism resulting from living in the presence of death and de-
struction, the breakdown of the usual middle-class moral standards, hungry women and girls prostituting themselves for a few
chocolate bars, cigarettes, or cakes of soap, and their children
or younger brothers at times pimping for them—it is easier to
comprehend the disruption subsequent to the Civil War of a

country which at best provided a bare subsistence for the vast majority. Cela's statement in the preface to the first edition of *La colmena* that ". . . today novels can be written—well or badly—only in the way I do it. If I thought the opposite, I should change my profession" is not boasting; it is an affirmation of the fact that he sees no other way to capture the bitter reality of Spanish life. He is in part proven right by the superiority of *La colmena* and *La familia de Pascual Duarte;* he could not write the usual trivial and ephemeral escapist literature. It is difficult to understand why some critics are surprised that his are the outstanding postwar novels.

Even very small sums of money assume an unusual importance as the solution to an immediate need. Several persons have money and, therefore, freedom and social position. Doña Rosa, one of the fortunate few, becomes brutal at the thought of losing the price of a cup of coffee. To Elvira, the fading prostitute, money means a decent meal or a package of small cigars. To Victoria it means medicine for her tubercular sweetheart. A few pesetas restore to the starving Seoane his self-confidence by allowing him to buy dark glasses for his suffering wife. To Martín a few pesetas here or there are a matter of life and death. Relative prosperity permits the printer Mario de Vega to condescend to give the impoverished college graduate a miserable job in his shop as well as to be able to purchase the favors of Victoria, whose sick fiancé has acquiesced in her prostitution. There is the little gypsy orphan who sings in the streets far into the morning to earn a handful of coppers. It is useless to go on. Behind nearly every act lies the question of money or lack of it, even in the case of the happily married couple who hesitate to make love, wondering whether they can afford to have another child.

The novel is not salacious or sensual since most sexual acts are performed rather prosaically with a desire for material gain. The explicit narration takes on a clinical aspect as the author focuses first on one situation and then another. It has been said that Spanish literature is not highly erotic, a generalization which seems to contradict the great realistic tradition (where there is no lack of compromising or equivocal situations), the voluptu-

ousness of Renaissance works, or the cultivation of foreign tendencies by Spanish imitators; but, as a rule, the observation is
quite true. The Spanish outlook on sensuality is tempered by
an objective, humorous, even picaresque and vulgar presentation which mitigates the carnal aspect and does not evoke a
vicarious sexual pleasure.

If nearly everyone in *La colmena* is concerned with money,
the same can be said of sex, except in the few cases where age
or special circumstances preclude it. Even non-participants profit
indirectly from sexual traffic; for instance, the children of Doña
Celia's niece cheer the arrival of couples at her house of assignation because it means they will eat the next day. Doña Celia
herself is lascivious and enjoys peeping through keyholes at the
lovers who rent her rooms (130, 217), and it is rumored that
the café owner, Doña Rosa, gets a secret pleasure from looking
at girls in their thin blouses and short sleeves (3). One of the
most humorous passages involves the homosexual Señor Suárez.
When the judge-magistrate interrogates a neighbor at the time
of his mother's murder, this dialogue ensues:

"Let's go step by step. Had the deceased any family?"

"Yes, Your Honor, a son."

"Where is he?"

"Pooh, how should anyone know? He's a man of bad habits, Your
Honor."

"A womanizer?"

"Well, no, Your Honor, not that."

"A gambler, maybe?"

"Well, no, not to my knowledge."

The magistrate looks at Don Ibrahim. "A drinker?"

"No, no, not a drinker either."

The magistrate forces a little smile.

"Tell me, then, what do you call bad habits? Collecting stamps?"

Don Ibrahim is piqued.

"No, sir, I call a number of things bad habits, for instance, being
a pansy."

"Ah, I see. The son of the deceased is a homosexual."

"Yes, Your Honor, a pansy through and through."

This interrogation provides humor as well as insight into

Don Ibrahim's character; earlier he has been portrayed as a pompous man rehearsing a speech (81-82). The comic dilemma of nearly everyone connected with the police inquiry into the mother's death, including that of the son himself, is effectively heightened by the macabre circumstances; besides serving as a focal point for the portrayal of certain characters, the investigation supplies the necessary contrast. Elsewhere the grimness of the narrative is lightened by amusing flashes which run the gamut of farce, jest, irony, and wit. In this manner Cela avoids the pitfalls of the novel of protest which takes itself too seriously. Life, no matter how harsh, furnishes an opportunity for laughter. In his various shades of comedy, Cela is in the great tradition of *The Celestina,* the picaresque novel, and *Don Quijote* in the sixteenth century, Galdós in the nineteenth century, and such writers of the Generation of 1898 as Baroja and Valle-Inclán.

Sex is the common denominator in *La colmena* just as it is in real life, and its variations go from perversion, matter-of-factness, young love with its illusions, to commercialism. The statement that here sex has the existentialist implications of the futile struggle against time[16] raises the question of such influence in *La colmena*. Individual conduct does not have to conform to essences or norms: the universe is irrational or absurd, the emptiness of life is filled with daily routine and mechanical action, and only man can resolve his own anguished existence. But there is lacking any reaction against absurdity, and the struggle to solve the limitations of time is absent. Fatalistic acceptance of one's lot is present to such an extent that man does not have the freedom to determine his own essence. Thus, existentialist tendencies in this novel are as greatly attenuated[17] as in *La familia de Pascual Duarte*.

Although there is sympathy for nearly all the personages, only in two instances does one react with really strong feelings of pity for the young girls involved. Merceditas, a girl of thirteen, walks hand in hand with Don Francisco, as though they were uncle and niece, toward Doña Celia's house of assignation. The child has lost her whole family in the war: some are dead, others in exile, and she must live with her grandmother's sister-in-law, Doña Carmen, nicknamed "Old Corpse Hair" or "Grass-hopper" by the children on the street.

Doña Carmen has sold Merceditas for five hundred pesetas, and Don Francisco, the one with the popular clinic, has bought her. She told the man: "First fruits, Don Francisco, first fruits. A carnation in bud."

And to the girl she said: "Look, child, all that Don Francisco wants is just to play. Anyway, it's got to happen one day, don't you see?" (230-31)

Don Francisco is a quack who advises against the use of the new sulfanilamides because he fears the loss of his practice; he is the father of numerous offspring, including Martín's friend, Nati (199-203). The usual compassion latent in Cela's blunt language is also completely lacking in his portrayal of the seminary student with the ludicrous name of Cojoncio Alba. Under pretext of showing the young girl Dorita some pictures of the life of St. Joseph of Calasanz, he leads her to a meadow and seduces her. The girl has a child. During the next vacation, the seminarist, later canon at León Cathedral, refuses to see her: "She's a wicked woman, . . . the spawn of the Evil One, and capable of dragging the most temperate man to perdition. . . . Let us avert our eyes from her" (235), with the result that her family abandons her. Don Francisco and the seminarist are "salauds" or rotters in the terminology of Sartre, and Cela's implication is that such persons have betrayed the trust of those for whose physical and spiritual well-being they are responsible.

The women in the novel seem to have more strength of character than the usually "sympathetically passive" men.[18] In the holocaust of the Civil War between 600,000 and 1,000,000 persons, mostly men, died, and about 400,000 went into exile.[19] It was inevitable that women in homes deprived of male influence would play a more independent role; it is historical irony that the great European wars in this century spawned social upheavals leading to greater emancipation for women. Spain for the first time went through such a cataclysm with the result that the traditional morality of the passive female was transformed,

even in families where there were still men; in the struggle for
the bare necessities of life the usual scruples were readily laid
aside. Spanish literature of the twentieth century already showed
a strong disposition away from the old melodramatic school
where a man's honor depended on a woman's chastity. Future
readers of Cela's novel may perhaps be more impressed by his
portrayal of Spain during this period of transition than by any
other aspect of the work.

La colmena is completely lacking in any depiction of physical
beauty; the settings are conceived of in ugliness, and there is
a remarkable dearth of references to physical attractiveness or
to its lack in a story where sex is so important.[20] But Cela is
not attempting to write the erotic novel; his is the clinical view.
Some of the younger women surely possess physical charm, but
Cela does not choose to emphasize it. Had he done so, the
whole tone, possibly even the structure, of the novel would be
different. Let us leave the last word to Cela. When he was
asked in an interview whether there were not virtuous, lovely
women and people without wens and anxieties, he replied:

I have been asked this question approximately fifteen or twenty thousand times. Of course, they exist, and we all know them. What happens is that they have no possible literary value. The novel of the
mild young man, besides being foolishness, is pernicious for society.
Nothing has caused more harm to the sensitivity of readers than rosy
novels or novels for young ladies.[21]

CHAPTER 7

Incest and Surrealism

I N 1953 Cela published *Mrs. Caldwell habla con su hijo,* a
work which he had slowly been accumulating—no other
word seems quite adequate—since the spring of 1947. Again he
uses a fragmentary technique, considerably more disjointed than
in *La colmena,* the epistolary jottings of a mad woman to her
son Eliacim, "tender as the leaf of maidenhair, who met death
heroically in the stormy waters of the Aegean Sea" (17) as a
result of enemy action.[1] In the Notice Cela assumes a matter-of-
fact tone and tells how he met the narrator at Pastrana on his
trip through the Alcarria as she was digging out the tiles in the
Princess of Eboli's deathchamber and stowing them away in
her suitcase. The tie-in with the capricious princess of the black
eyepatch and uninhibited correspondence may be more than
fortuitous on the author's part; one reference to the transmigration of souls has been noted in his *Lazarillo* and he will take up
metempsychosis anew in later works.

In compliance with her last request, the final manuscript is
sent to him upon Mrs. Caldwell's death in the Royal Hospital
for the Insane. Such preliminary information hardly strikes the
reader as stylistic novelty. Certain critics fail to see any realistic
characterization of the lady of the title,[2] and upon looking back
at the Notice, one finds that Mrs. Caldwell is perhaps most
recognizable at this point where she stands out as a kind of
eccentric Englishwoman wandering around the world as an ex-
patriate, living on occasion through harrowing circumstances.
Cela was certainly not unequipped to create such a woman in
the conventional mold if he had wished; the suggestion for the
type could easily have come to him from some of his English

aunts on his mother's side of the family, whom he had met in England. Instead, he chose to present the disconnected, illogical notes of an unbalanced woman. Those who dismiss or ignore *Mrs. Caldwell* in a study of his works do so arbitrarily, but admittedly there are difficulties of interpretation. It represents his "fifth approach to the technique of writing novels . . ." (10), and he writes it in the second person to the extent that such is possible without confusing the reader (14). Since it is not a novel by any customary definition, Cela, with irony, broadens the term to include "everything published in the form of a book which can accept under the title, and in parentheses, the word 'novel'" (9). The work is about as much an anti-novel as has yet been conceived in Spain. An imperceptive critic might find *Mrs. Caldwell* only the excuse for presenting the author's notebook jottings in a unique manner. It is in as sharp contrast with *La colmena* as *Pabellón de reposo* is with *La familia de Pascual Duarte*.

I *Thwarted Maternal Instincts*

There is no denying the esteem Cela has for this novel, a feeling reiterated in the prologue to *Mis páginas preferidas* (147) and in personal conversations with me. Ilie's study on Cela[3] dedicates more space to an analysis of *Mrs. Caldwell* than to any of the other novels; with some reservations, one can accept his observations on its incestuous and surrealistic tendencies. Cela states rather enigmatically in his foreword that "it would be a bad idea . . . to get into the fix of saying where the key to my book may be hidden, or whether my book . . . has any key at all" (13). He may be playing games; yet a key is no more necessary here than it is to explain an abstract painting. By not looking for such an explanatory device or demanding the usual structure, one can read the selections of widely varying length for their stylistic innovation, humor, bizarre combination of ideas, and poetry. Some critical opinion has even classified the work as primarily lyrical;[4] there is no objection to such an approach, but it does not enable us to cope with the challenge presented by the content.

Mrs. Caldwell is mentally unbalanced, but nothing more un-clinical than the consideration of her character can be imagined. Her aberrations permit the random attribution of all kinds of thoughts, sometimes even in the form of dreams. Is she meant to be portrayed as a possessive mother whose maternal instincts are complicated by incestuous inclinations? Ilie does not analyze Mrs. Caldwell in the usual Freudian terms, but his findings confirm such an interpretation.[5] There are a number of allusions to unsatisfactory relations, sexual and otherwise, between Mrs. Caldwell and her husband. She refers to him ironically (q. D. h. —"God rest his soul"), and describes almost humorously his posture in death—she gave him only a second-class funeral although the neighbor and rival who cuckolded him would have made up the difference (24, 54). Significantly, he had suffered from phimosis, which made sexual relations difficult. In general, Mrs. Caldwell takes a dim view of matrimony "which kills love or at least wounds it seriously" (85), and in certain symbolic passages shows a tendency to assume a masculine role in the home. Her attitude toward her own father is also ambiguous, and quite early she seems to have developed guilt feelings toward him.[6] She compensates for her unsatisfactory married life by centering all her attention on her son.[7] After he is lost to her, she is consumed by guilt because of her supposed pernicious influence on him, because of his abandonment of her, and because of her illicit love for him.[8] Her personality, then, combines aggressiveness and a guilt complex.

In the selection entitled "Lord Macaulay," we learn that the birth of her son was the result of adulterous relations—an unimportant factor—since in comparison with the all-encompassing love of a mother, the role of the father is trivial. She would have liked that Eliacim possess the excellent qualities of Lord Macaulay, who would have made the boy a wonderful mother. "Being your father, he would only have fulfilled his duty. But . . . time is something against which I have not yet discovered any way to fight" (55).

Her thoughts on "Maternal Instinct" illustrate her attitude quite well.[9] The usual edifying concept of maternity is rather suspect, but it reveals a heretofore unnoticed facet of her nature: Mrs. Caldwell unconsciously resents her illegitimate son, a feeling easy to control until his untimely end. She has no reason to feel guilt about his "heroic death in the stormy waters of the Aegean."[10] After all, he died bravely fighting against a ruthless enemy of his country, this being an action in which any English mother could find consolation. But to her such sentiments are only a vulgar display. One can hardly see in Mrs. Caldwell an allegory of a grieving Spain speaking to the sons who have died in the Civil War.[11] Nevertheless, Cela's stressing of the wartime death at the outset remains ambiguous, unless it is dismissed merely as a nicely turned phrase. Her reflections are quoted at length:

Maternal instinct, my beloved son, is something much less abstruse than people think, something much easier, perhaps, to guess than to understand. Maternal instinct, Eliacim, is often painted with an overglaze of bronze or smoke in order not to have to present, shamelessly, its face. The maternal instinct, son, is something which it seems should be hidden, something to be veiled modestly.

The spider, my son, is, among all the animals, the one which most sharply exhibits the maternal instinct, disguising itself frequently as a flower in the field or stag in the woods in order not to have to explain its strange customs all the time.

Among women, Eliacim, and your mother has been one for a good many years now, the maternal instinct has been hidden beneath the thick veneer of good breeding. That is probably bad, but such is the case.

I noticed—don't tell anyone—that I couldn't avoid the maternal instinct, the very day you put on your first long trousers, gray trousers in the style of the Prince of Wales, in which you were resplendent.

Until then, I had always thought that the maternal instinct was a topic applicable to married women of the middle and lower classes. (96-97)

Mrs. Caldwell holds up to view in a quite explicit manner the rational and apparently irrational sides of her personality. Her words reflect loathing for the commonplace women—all mothers —around the swimming pool who occasionally pause to urinate in the water until inhibited by the addition of a special chemical that turns red in urine (33-34); her contempt for middle-class women is echoed in "The Strangest and Most Wholesome Women" (142-43), where she finds in typical manner that they ". . . usually have a nest of scorpions in their bosom, a seething mass of scorpions pulsating in their elevated and powerful bosom."

We are now beginning to understand Mrs. Caldwell's inner conflict somewhat better. She has a snobbish disdain for motherhood as it ordinarily manifests itself, complicated by certain guilt feelings, but neither can she escape the maternal condition. Her irrational, even lyrical, references to spiders and scorpions are an expression of her dislike for the benignly appearing predatory instincts of mothers everywhere. This imagery recalls that for Cela the spider is also a symbol of maternal sacrifice. Note how in the following lines he relates the spider to himself, a detail that leads one to seek in *Mrs. Caldwell* some of those most intimate thoughts he refers to on occasion:

The spider, the delicate and maternal spider, should be the totem animal of the writer. Nobody except the spider—and the writer—is capable of opening the belly so that hungry offspring may devour her. (*Páginas preferidas,* p. 409)

Mrs. Caldwell never has kind words for motherhood. There are vague implications that the work is "a satire on what we believe to be the loftiest of human feelings, maternal love. If this be the case, Mrs. Caldwell might well be the incarnation of Pascual Duarte's mother. Insanity may be a more cruel fate than death."[12] Pascual Duarte's mother is unforgettable and, like the mother of Cela's Lazarillo, seems to be practically devoid of the usual parental sentiments. In *La colmena* a number of mothers appear in important, typical, but not always sympathetic roles, and the protagonist in Part II of *La Catira* is motivated by maternal instincts more than anything else, insofar as can be determined from the sketchy characterization. The theme of motherhood in all of Cela's works is worthy of a more detailed study. The impact of *Mrs. Caldwell* comes partly from the fact that we are conditioned to venerate the institutions of home and mother.

Cela is above all a Spanish writer true to the psychology of his people, and while mothers may be basically the same everywhere, he could make observations about Spanish motherhood in his portrayal of the eccentric Englishwoman without provoking an unduly hostile reaction from the reading public or government censorship. In "It Is All Quite Simple" (201), Mrs. Caldwell expresses her frustration with the inescapable female role: "A woman is born, grows up, gets married, goes shopping, has a son, more or less keeps house, loses her son, goes in for charitable works, is bored, and dies." The life role of the man, however, is no less absurd:

A man is born, grows up, learns a profession, gets married, tries to earn more money every day, has a son, goes to the club in the afternoon, loses his son, tells tremendous lies about the war or his hunting in Tanganyika, is bored, dies. And thus, once, twice, three, four times.

Except for a minor point here and there, such is the universal pattern of life.

The problem faced by some young men is how to emancipate themselves from maternal domination. On one occasion Eliacim's mother lists three of his basic attitudes toward her: he is friendly toward everything surrounding her, but isolates her "in a cold island of indifference"; she is an obstacle in his life; and finally he wishes, quite frankly, that she were dead (178). The more Mrs. Caldwell "pretends to be engulfed in the life of her son, the more she tells about her own experience." [13] The boy is never portrayed as having a personality of his own, but Cela probably makes him an abstraction deliberately. In novels there are often detailed accounts of the relationship between two people, but seldom, if ever, is one of them dead.

At times Mrs. Caldwell voices the most commonplace motherly sentiments. When Eliacim is allowed to smoke his first cigarette, she is ". . . about to burst out crying from sadness, . . . like a woman very much in love with her husband who has just received word by telephone that she has suddenly been left a widow" (128); yet in a later parallel passage she adds, "I could hardly keep from crying with enthusiasm, like a re-

pentant, sinful woman" (129). Her first reaction is that of a
typical mother, but the second indicates that, with increasing
manhood, Eliacim becomes a substitute for her deceased husband. If military service had not intervened, the son would
have found it difficult ever to escape from her control. In all
of Mrs. Caldwell's utterances one is aware that she does not
accept his death with any sort of resignation, Christian or otherwise. Almost to the end she speaks of his desertion (185, 215).
That she is obviously a woman of unusual qualities helps to
explain her condescension or distaste for most other women.
What will happen to her when she finally admits to herself
that her son is irrevocably gone? When her already unstable
mind has to accept his loss, there is nothing left for her but
hopeless insanity and death.

Her demise of course is hastened by tuberculosis (191).
Friends and an alienist visit her at home and recommend that
she enter a sanitarium for rest (213-17). Before leaving the
"inhospitable, repulsive, treacherous home" (217-18), she claims
to have erased all memory of her son and declares that if she
had the courage and time, she would burn down the house
itself. Evidently attendants or friends get to her just in time
to prevent this desperate, mad act.

Four short selections, "Air," "Earth," "Fire," and "Water" (219-
22), bring the novel to its highly symbolic conclusion. In the
first, Mrs. Caldwell thinks her room is filled with pressurized
air, "like in tires, enough air to breathe for a whole lifetime."
In the second, she has planted more than a thousand tuberose
shoots, and she finds her room filling with earth. If Eliacim
were only with her, she would bury him every night—she does
not sleep—under the washbasin and dig him up in the morning
so he could breathe. "And when the earth filled the whole room,
we two would die, my love, in an eternal embrace." In the passage "Fire," she speaks of undressing in her flame-filled room
before her son, who is taking notes—an unpleasant prospect
since she is aging. To please him, she has spent the whole day
dressing and undressing with vertiginous rapidity. She uses the
sexual symbols of a tail and horns. She realizes also that her
friends never come to visit her any more and that they must

suspect she is in some sort of dangerous place. The final selection breaks off after nine lines when Mrs. Caldwell's room fills with water. Hers is a cosmic death, and somewhere she may be reunited with her son.

The use of the four elements to present death in an attractive manner may recall certain parallels of imagery from a poem by Juan Ramón Jiménez.[14]

> That was all. Not the slightest
> trace (brand or cinder)
> of anything in the depths.
> Nor the most fluid
> flight of anything throughout the
> encircling all. Nor in its place,
> the vaguest reflection of life or death
> behind the silver of the mirror
> of a spectral kind.
>
> . . . Throughout the air and the earth
> a something I know not what of fire or water.

> (*No fué más. Ni el más leve*
> *rastro (tizo o escoria)*
> *en el fondo de nada.*
> *Ni el más flúido*
> *vuelo de nada por el ámbito*
> *de todo. Ni, en su sitio,*
> *el más vago revés de vida o muerte*
> *tras el azogue del espejo*
> *de lo espectral.*
>
> *. . . Por el aire y la tierra,*
> *no sé qué fuego o agua.*)

Cela states in a note that the last two pages of the manuscript sent to him were smeared and illegible, showing traces of dampness as though having been submerged for several hours. Whether one reacts favorably or unfavorably to *Mrs. Caldwell,* he cannot deny that Cela found a fitting way to portray the death of an extraordinary woman.

II *Fragmented Reality*

Mrs. Caldwall habla con su hijo is not a work that has a structured plot or story progression, even though it is possible to make observations about the single character as we have just done. Mrs. Caldwell speaks of a number of persons and frequently of her son, but the writer of these confessions, broken up into 212 selections, each averaging a little over a page in length, is the protagonist and only real person in the novel. It would be possible to read the short entries in any order, except, perhaps, for the last four, even though she becomes somewhat more irrational in the later parts of the book. In a note to the excerpts from *Mrs. Caldwell,* chosen for *Mis páginas preferidas* (147), Cela calls it a work from his more authentic and daring poetic vein in whose imagery the reader should be prepared to see an irrationality well suited to the form.

One incident will illustrate his technique of taking a realistic situation to which he adds the hypothetical but related elements to be found in any fiction as well as lyric touches associated with the mental processes of Mrs. Caldwell—all tied to the principal theme, the loss of her son. She speaks of the street musicians—players of the cornet, accordion, and violin—who perform at the doors of taverns or entrances to churches in honor of young newlyweds without the means of earning a livelihood. So far, the presentation is factual and somewhat nostalgic. Then she has the idea of taking the musicians into her large house.

. . . in it would fit your mother and her street musicians, her warm, aromatic street musicians, who wear caps with oilcloth visors and have a lyre tattooed over their hearts. . . .

Yes, Eliacim, if it wouldn't cause talk, I would fill our house with street musicians on April 17, your birthday; they would agree gladly to play at the door of your empty room the pieces that you might like best. (165-66)

Here the sequence is logical, but verging on irrationality. The lyre tattooed over the musicians' hearts is both appropriate and striking imagery.

In one of the longest chapters, Mrs. Caldwell takes inventory of her belongings before entering the sanitarium. She has consented to be hospitalized because she wants to recover her health so that she may ". . . keep living, my son, in order to continue loving you and remembering you constantly" (216). Then she narrates a surrealistic dream filled with symbolism.

Last night I dreamed I was entering a store, a large department store, to buy myself a boy doll. It was something I had needed to do for a long time, although I was always very much ashamed, inexplicably ashamed, of the idea of going to the toy section, the doll section, to tell the clerk, "I want a boy doll as perfect as possible, the price doesn't matter." Once in the store I took a long time to make up my mind, because, really there wasn't any boy doll that I liked completely. After turning the store upside down, Eliacim, I chose one which looked like the clerk. "This one, give me this one, please." The clerk looked at me, son, going under the light so I could see him better, and I could not contain a shout. I fell to the floor, people flocked around, and they brought me a glass of water. "My son, my son, I have just seen my son Eliacim!" The clerk, elbowing his way through the crowd, fled to the street and went and hid in a brothel, under a bed which had a red silk coverlet like our curtain. I began to lose weight and more weight, son, until I was finally changed into a dove without eyes. I flew to a roof, and there, at the foot of a chimney, laid a small egg, round and pink-colored. (216-17)

A dream imagined by a writer, unlike the real thing, is a literary creation that permits analysis to show the relation of elements brought together for the author's purposes. There is a plausible explanation,[15] but it can be simplified and related to other themes in the book. Because of grief for her lost son, frustrated maternal instincts, and amorous desires, it is not surprising that Mrs. Caldwell would purchase a boy doll. The fusion of images doll-boy, child-companion, clerk-father-companion in games is understandable in terms of sexuality, with the clerk cast first in the husband's role. The flight of the clerk to the brothel recalls the desertion by her son that Mrs. Caldwell speaks of earlier. She was jealous of Eliacim's marble figurine of a Chinese prostitute (176-78), and so, in her opinion, an interest in any woman other than herself is reprehensible. The allusion to the red curtain, one of the few cross-references, recalls her description of the old drapery on which she customarily dried her eyes (197-98). She has been saddened to think of the curtain, like everything else around her, aging and coming to pieces, since her playful child was accustomed to hide behind it. Now it is symbolically lost in the house of prostitution, as are her son and his innocence. Among other possible interpretations, her transformation into a blind dove as an escape from reality and the laying of the egg as a realization of maternal instinct—even though the egg may be whimsy on Cela's part—seem to be pertinent. The chimney would symbolize hearth and home and a yearning for domestic felicity.

By concentrating on Mrs. Caldwell, it is possible that an impression has been given that the work possesses a thematic intensity which, in reality, it lacks. In *Mis páginas preferidas,* Cela identifies himself more closely with the lady and also gives us a clue to what he was about: "If I had been born a woman, I would probably have had my mind organized—or disorganized—like my sensitive and good friend Mrs. Caldwell, an adorable woman, although perhaps a bit unusual" (147). The humorous vein often lying just beneath the surface of his writing is typical.

By taking from the index ten titles at random—"Music Hall," "A Tango from the Old Days," "Cognac and Rum," "The Cog Railway," "The Flies," "The Trout," "The Hourglass," "Argot," "The Clouds," "Bronze Paperweights"—and then turning to the pages indicated, one discovers that Mrs. Caldwell holds forth to Eliacim on these varied topics, on a personal note in keeping with her presumed character. Nevertheless, they could be omitted without greatly affecting the whole work. Or else, Cela might have written notes on these topics frankly directed to the general public, as he does in later collections of miscellaneous essays. But had he done so, they would have lost something of the strangeness and intimacy which heighten their effect. One of the attractions of a novel is that the reader is carried along by his involvement with the protagonists and their problems. Mrs. Caldwell and her rather shadowy son provide the reader with the slender thread of story needed to prevent his putting the book down unfinished, as might well happen with a collection of jottings, however well written. Any method an author employs to encourage continued reading is legitimate as long as a conclusion consistent with the content is provided. Cela supplies this essential and therefore can rightly call this work a novel.

CHAPTER 8

The Wide Open Spaces

CELA'S approach to the llanos of Venezuela in *La Catira* (1955) recalls the incomprehension of those foreign journalistic accounts about the Middle West and Western United States found in the "Five Months in the United States" sort of chronicle, except that in his book he has tried conscientiously to capture something of the overwhelming nature of the open grasslands—the unifying theme, in fact, of the novel. Nevertheless, a few months in a country and a literary style bristling with problematical Venezuelan Americanisms—a glossary of 896 terms is appended—are no susbstitute for prolonged recollection and an ear for speech cadences which even a native has to grasp at times almost intuitively.

I *El Dorado at Last*

In 1954 Cela was declared Guest of Honor of Venezuela and commissioned to write a novel with that country as the setting. The author has brushed off those who asked him how much money he received for his effort with the remark, "More than my enemies say, much more, and somewhat less than my optimistic creditors say." [1] The novel received favorable attention from a number of critics, particularly from those who had been frustrated by *Mrs. Caldwell habla con su hijo*; but there was no lack of detractors. [2] In the foreword to the selections chosen from *La Catira* for *Mis páginas preferidas* (179), Cela states what he has attempted to do:

La Catira is, according to my intention, an impassioned hymn to the Venezuelan woman. Also to the Venezuelan land. At times love does

114

not find expressions with which to make itself understood. This is a "novelistic" novel, [one] with a great deal of action, much passion, and no little poetry—although I don't know whether it is effective or not. In *La Catira* I tried, with all sorts of vexations, the double experiment of incorporating the American world and its special language into Spanish literature. . . .

This passage serves well as the point of departure for a discussion of the work.

The heroine Pipía Sánchez—"Pipía" is short for the symbolic Primitiva—although a woman capable of violent action, is essentially good. At the story's beginning, she flees the ranch of her supposed father, Don Froilán—in the process shooting a peon without compunction—to go to the neighboring ranch of Don Filiberto. She appears to be motivated more by a desire to escape from her father than by her love for Filiberto because she tells him: "If you don't want me in Potreritos, there'll be some half-breed who'll take me in" (27).[3] Their prompt marriage brings on a range war between Don Filiberto and Don Froilán (not actually her father, but the one who had killed her real father, who was the lover of Froilán's faithless wife).

Without too much difficulty Don Filiberto and his men defend the ranch against Don Froilán's attack, but for unexplained reasons the defenders make a sortie to catch the attackers from the rear and are unexpectedly caught in ambush and butchered. These poorly motivated actions are presented without any statement of the tactics involved. The unfortunate turn of events is accounted for only by a Spanish proverb "las cañas se tornaron lanzas," "the tables were turned" (44). Even mediocre writers of novels dealing with the Far West or the pampas of Argentina employ a plausible formula for such a maneuver.

After the death of her recently acquired husband, La Catira rides out alone to confront Don Froilán, saying: "If my papa wants, he will strike my face with his whip . . . he will drag me by the hair across the whole prairie . . ." (47). Things happen as she predicts. Her initial acceptance of such treatment as just is presumably meant to show that as a primitive creature she expects to be punished for filial disobedience. But when Don Froilán attempts to trample her under his horse's hooves,

she fires six shots from her revolver into his body and " . . .
didn't miss once" (48).

The remainder of Part I has relatively little to do with La
Catira, except to show rather vaguely her attempt to run the
two ranches she has inherited and her gallops across the llanos
in occasional displays of energy. Most of the action comes from
Don Juan Evangelista Pacheco, Don Filiberto's old companion,
and his men who pursue a horse thief, Aquiles Valles, through
most of Venezuela's back country. Their wanderings permit the
author to bring in a lot of geography and presumably give epic
proportions to the novel. Eventually Juan Evangelista encounters an itinerant Galician, Evaristo Sarela Pazos, who, like Cela
himself, is from Iria near Padrón.

One chapter, entitled "La caribera" ("The Piranha Pool"),
describes a stream infested with piranha capable of devouring
man and beast. There are occasional scenes showing the activities of Aquiles Valles and his two companions. Once, while his
two associates rape an Indian woman, the perverted Aquiles
prefers to gratify himself by beating the husband to death (97).
Cela possibly reaches the peak of his "tremendista" tendencies
in a later scene showing Valles' homosexual attack on his companion Gilberto Flores, killing him when he resists, and then,
in an act of necrophilia, ravishing the body (144). The pur-
suers close in on Valles and he dies horribly after falling into
the stream swarming with the cannibal fish. This finale is not
without a grotesque humor: Evaristo, the Galician, who earlier
has said that he does not know how to shoot a gun, fires at
Valles, misses him, but hits the horse in the mouth so that it
dumps the rider into the stream (170-72). This accumulation
of horrors is likely to produce laughter in any but the most
squeamish reader. Unfortunately, more is yet to come. As the
men return to La Catira's ranch, a jaguar jumps Pacheco and
wounds him in the shoulder before he can kill it; they strike a
light to look at the dead beast and it appears to have the scarred
face of the late Don Froilán. This unexpected turn of events
causes the befuddled reader to wonder as to the author's intention.

If Part I is the ultimate in gory action, by contrast the second part moves uneventfully, too much so, in fact. Some fifteen or sixteen years have passed. Pacheco meanwhile has returned from his wanderings (he has ridden off with the Galician Evaristo at the close of Part I), acquires a ranch of his own, and marries La Catira. A son is born to them. Soon afterwards, Pacheco is killed by a fall from the hammock where he has been napping when his spur gets caught in the net, and Pipía is once again a widow. Now she has four ranches to manage: she has two at the time of her marriage to Pacheco, she inherits one from him, and she buys one belonging to the two sisters who are cousins of the first husband. Since we never see her actually engaged in serious ranching, just how she goes about managing such a large estate is uncertain. She says something about combining all the properties and ordering a new brand for the whole spread (235), but there is a lot more to ranching than idle chit-chat with domestics or drinking iced whisky, as is her habit.

Most of Part II is filled with anecdotes, legends, rather dull sketches of local customs, and the antics of three brothers: Feliciano Bujanda, foreman of La Catira's ranch; Publio, owner of the ice cream factory in Maracaibo; and Leónidas who writes songs for Saludable Fernández, renowned locally as a singer of popular songs, whose thrice-married sister Telefoníasinhilos (Wirelesstelegraphy) is about to have her ninth child. Most of the children have names as strange as the mother's.

II *Encroaching Progress*

After Pacheco's death, La Catira will not allow her son to ride horses. She awaits the arrival of Miss Fanny, an "americanita" twenty years old, from Atlanta, to teach "manners, reading, and writing" to the young Juan Evangelista (259-60). On the way to the airport to meet Miss Fanny, Feliciano Bujanda, driver of the jeep, and his companion, Juan Evangelista, strike a bull and both are killed (300). Simultaneous happenings are presented with the now familiar technique of jumping from one scene to another: at the ranch La Catira prepares to receive Miss Fanny; Publio Bujanda and his mistress Saludable Fernández—sometimes called "The Cuban Tornado"—are on their

way to meet her sister and husband; the boy and foreman
proceed to the airport.

The journey of Publio and Saludable is interrupted by an
interlude of love-making; that of her sister and husband by
an account of their driver who lacks an ear, but is able to blow
smoke out of the place where it was. The two couples fail to
meet at the appointed place; when Publio and his lady friend
set out on the highway to find the lost sister and her husband,
they all eventually come together at the site of the accident.
They take the bodies of the son and driver back to the ranch,
where, before realizing that anything is wrong, musicians start
playing "Soul of the Llanos" and a peon shouts, "Long live the
gringa Miss Fanny, a new citizen of the state of Guárico . . . !"
(324).

It is really difficult to know how to evaluate this novel,
and even harder to understand how critics can take it seriously.
That Cela performs feats of linguistic manipulation is undeniable. It has even been the subject of a lengthy monograph of
stylistic analysis.[4] Cela's earlier remark that, when one writes
what others wish, he is no longer a writer,[5] calls to mind the
circumstances under which this work was composed. One is
equally puzzled to learn that it received the Premio de la
Crítica award in 1956.[6] Confidence in the many Spanish literary
prizes is hardly strengthened by the fact that none of Cela's
earlier works had received such distinction. This sensational
book may have reminded literary juries that Cela was overdue
for an award and that it would be a nice gesture of international good will toward Venezuela. Much more depressing is
the thought that Spaniards failed to see in La Catira an exploi-
tation of their own stereotyped concept of South America.

It has been pointed out that even educated people in the
story, such as the priest or Pacheco, speak an illiterate jargon
of dubious Venezuelan Spanish.[7] Inevitably La Catira has been
compared to Rómulo Gallegos' Doña Bárbara about the Venezuelan llanos—one of the best South American novels—but
resemblances between the two are rather casual. One must stress
the authenticity of language in Doña Bárbara; the hero, Santos
Luzardo, is a man of some education whose precise speech is,

on occasion, confusing to a country girl. In *La Catira*, Cela's orthography, more than the language he uses, presents the problem: his attempt to portray the South American pronunciation is distracting until one becomes accustomed to his system. The main linguistic defect, however, is the lack of suitable nuances between the speech of people of different social levels or personality. Cela constantly uses a form of reiteration that has become his trademark, although it existed to a lesser degree in earlier writers like Baroja and Azorín. The use of this device —a sort of anaphora usually involving a person's name—may be quite effective with childlike or primitive characters,[8] but it becomes monotonous when repeated on any number of pages. For instance,

Catalino Borrego showed his age. Catalino Borrego's face was lined, as a razor marks wood, with furrows. Catalino Borrego had white hair. Catalino Borrego no longer wrestled steers, nor ran races, nor danced. Catalino Borrego trained fighting cocks, played the harp and dominoes. Catalino Borrego knew only too well why La Catira Pipía Sánchez had not given him the job of casting the brand of La Pachequera. (255)

There is a kind of murky symbolism in the boy's death in the jeep accident, the idea evidently being that he would have been much safer around horses than in modern vehicles of foreign import. The fact that the accident occurs while the foreman and the boy are on their way to the airport to meet Miss Fanny, who will teach the lad English, reinforces this interpretation, just as does the discussion on modern progress between Saludable and her sister on the ride back to the ranch with the two corpses. Saludable stresses the innovations in Maracaibo of television and baseball, and the sister counters that her home town has all that and even more (323). The place for a future rancher, then, is on his land where he can be trained for his true vocation. In the final chapter the author tries to unite the two themes, the Venezuelan woman and the land, which he claims inspired the novel. After her son's death it is rumored that La Catira will sell her ranches and leave. The priest remarks to her: "Look, Catira, the land is left, see?

The land is the main thing, Catira, everything else is nonsense and mere waste of time" (339). And he repeats like a litany, "The land always remains."

Because Pipía is so closely bound to the earth, she becomes a kind of fertility symbol. The maid María del Aire offers to give her the baby she is carrying in her womb, fruit of her love for the dead foreman. La Catira is touched by the offer and, at the same time, her vanity is wounded. She thinks herself not too old to produce her own child; she will go even as far as Caracas if necessary to find a father for a future son and heir because, she repeats to the Negress, ". . . the land is left, woman . . . the land always remains, see?" The similarities and contrasts between the two women—one looking forward to the birth of a child, the other pining for a dead son—provide a moment of valid insight into the feminine mentality that calls to mind Cela's interest in and talent for portraying maternal figures. The novel closes with La Catira seated, nude, before her mirror murmuring, ". . . the land has to be made of the same blood that brought it peace. . . . Yes . . . ."

Cela momentarily comes to grips at the conclusion with a force that has been there all along so that briefly the story takes on the breadth he had planned. In spite of the poorly motivated violence of Part I, his overdrawn characterization of La Catira could have been a striking literary creation; instead, he dissipates his fundamental plot in a welter of factitious, disparate elements that only lend support to the argument that he is incapable of writing a novel with sustained narrative and fully developed protagonists. Up to now, such criticism has largely been unwarranted. Cela would not be worthy of a detailed study if he were only a writer of mediocre, conventional novels. In *La Catira* he is unfortunately never able to adopt a form to fit the content because it is never clear to him just what that form should be. When he fails to write a " 'novelistic' novel—one with a great deal of action, much passion, and no little poetry," the reader must conclude that either he did not decide clearly what was involved or that, more likely, he wrote the prologue after the book was completed and by then it was too late. When one remembers that passable adven-

ture yarns are written with considerable speed, it does not help
to say that this novel of 357 pages—not counting the glossary
—was written hastily. Its ambiguous nature is underscored by
the subtitle *Historias de Venezuela* (*Venezuelan Stories*), re-
minding us of a basic anecdotal tendency from which he was
unable to escape. Yet Cela is to be admired; he has the talent
to make a good living as a writer—something rare with Spanish
authors.

This study of the not entirely successful *La Catira* is useful
because it permits an appreciation of Cela's accomplishments
in his earlier novels, however much one may quibble over the
position they must occupy as examples of the genre. Looking
back no farther than *Mrs. Caldwell habla con su hijo*, the reader
is reassured that in it Cela is at least not parodying himself
in a milieu he does not entirely apprehend.

CHAPTER 9

Books of Vagabondage

AFTER having considered the debatable merits of *La Catira*, one turns with pleasure to *Viaje a la Alcarria* (1948), the first and perhaps best of Cela's narratives about his walking tours through various regions of Spain. This material was recorded in notebooks during the period June 6-15, 1946, and put into final form at the end of 1947. The author's almost hourly account of what happens and what he sees during this excursion through a district only forty miles northeast of Madrid has been received favorably by Spanish critics, and since the whole outing was uneventful, the artistic accomplishment is all the more remarkable.

I *Eloquent Silence*

Cela's aesthetic achievement is possibly best expressed by one critic who quotes Claudel to the effect that a poem is made not only with letters, but also with the white spaces left on the page:

This whiteness is silence and the active listening of the poet. If one writes a book on the Alcarria, he has to listen to the Alcarria. . . . Although one may say certain things, what speaks underneath is the Alcarria.[1]

"Immerse oneself in the people," Unamuno exhorted, and he coined the term "infrahistoria," to mean the submerged, unrecorded tradition of the humble; but Unamuno was too loquacious to listen very much. Not so Cela.

Despite his personal experiences, Cela paradoxically makes his presence in the narrative unobtrusive by calling himself

"the traveler" and allowing persons and places visited to speak
for themselves. Such self-restraint is extraordinary in a writer
with as strongly marked a personality as his; he remains dis-
creetly silent even in encounters with people who at the very
least would provoke comical distortion. For example, Cela speaks
casually, and only in the Dedication, of his imprisonment for
a day and night in a small-town jail by an obnoxious mayor—
a drunken, stammering albino—who, on other occasions, would
have supplied him with sufficient notes for an etching.

This book is not a novel, Cela comments further; it is geography, without the usual encyclopedic data. He captures the
tone of the work in his dedicatory lines to Gregorio Marañón:
"I am sending you a flower which I picked in a roadside ditch;
all this time I have had it placed in a book and now it is dried.
I think it is pretty" (IV, 28).

In Chapter 1 something is said of the circumstances surrounding Cela's wanderings. Walking quite possibly had been
recommended for his tubercular condition. There is the brief
short story of 1947, only recently accessible, about a taciturn,
pallid little man who is advised vaguely by his doctor to take
walks for his health "during a suitable time. . . . At a healthy
hour" (II, 326), and who then walks the thirty miles from
Madrid to the Escorial and back. His café friends, however,
do not believe his story, and to prove his point he walks to
Zaragoza and back, a distance which takes two months. His
friends are even more incredulous and think him "completely
mad." The little man goes home in disgust. They later decide
to pay him a visit, and learn from his wife—he is asleep—that,
because they will not listen to or believe his stories, he is
threatening to walk all the way to the Holy Land. The next
day in the café they beg to hear about his trip to Zaragoza.
"And our fellow breathed peacefully, told them about Zaragoza,
and began to forget all about the Holy Land" (II, 328).

The author's road to the Alcarria also lies on the way to
Zaragoza, the destination of most travelers passing through the
region, just as it was for the Cid and his men nearly nine
centuries before. The Arabic name means "the village (or country) of huts," and now serves to designate the high, flat *páramos*

located at an altitude of over three thousand feet, cut by three
rivers, the Tajo, Tajuña, and Guadiela, to form relatively fertile, narrow bottoms some three hundred feet lower down. In
the occasional fertile *vegas* the thick green vegetation and dark
poplars contrast with the golden, white, or reddish earth of
the slopes and tops. Covered mostly by scrubby aromatic bushes
and plants from whose flowers the bees make the honey for
which the province is noted, the slopes are dotted here and
there with olives and live oaks. The small villages seek shelter
from the cold winter winds on slopes near the little prairies,
and none of the four main towns—Brihuega, Cifuentes, Sacedón,
and Pastrana—has more than four thousand inhabitants.[2]

Here, as in the old Castilian town of Cebreros, Cela approaches the area without preconceived sentiments or aesthetic
preoccupations. In this region on the outskirts of Madrid he
discovers a world overlooked by city dwellers and transforms
its routine provincial life into literature—a fact which possibly
explains why the account has impressed most Spanish readers.
The author makes elaborate preliminary plans for the excursion, mapping routes and calculating distances, but once in
Guadalajara his itinerary becomes a series of random hikes of
from twelve to fifteen miles a day.

It must be emphasized that the sights he views are of slight
importance: an old castle, an abandoned factory with a charming garden, manor houses with heraldic shields, and portals
with wrought-iron fittings. Such things are to be seen anywhere
in Spain. Here they serve more as props or background for a
sensitive portrayal of the people he meets: numerous children,
village idiots, inns, and the men, women, and girls who run
them; an itinerant jack-of-all-trades, shepherds, an occasional
shopkeeper, a wagoner who takes wood into Guadalajara every
morning, a traveling salesman on bicycle, and so on; and, of
course, the road and countryside with its heat, flowers, animals, birds, insects, and other fauna. Appropriately enough, he
cites at the beginning these lines from William Cullen Bryant:
"To him who in the love of nature holds / Communion with
her visible forms, she speaks / A various language" (IV, 25).

The Alcarria would not furnish to many writers very promising material from which to fashion a minor masterpiece, especially when the author makes no attempt to infuse it with any subjective, lyrical spirit—except for unpretentious little stanzas of popular verse which go so well with this low-keyed work. What gives the account its appeal—and in this respect Cela surpasses the old *costumbrista* and the more artistically pretentious writers of the Generation of 1898—is his artless portrayal of the persons he encounters, on whose same level he places himself by traveling on foot with practically no money in his pockets. More often than not, local people accept the wanderer. And, in this manner, he establishes bonds with them as no passing visitor in search of folklore or picturesqueness could ever do, who, by the very nature of such a quest, would be unable to avoid an involuntary patronizing attitude toward these more or less colorful rustics.

The people in *Viaje a la Alcarria*, living or fictional, are so real that Cela keeps in touch with some of them and adds more details about their lives in the two later collections of *Los viejos amigos*. In the dialogue with the crackbrained shopkeeper Julio Vacas, who also shows visitors around Brihuega, Cela speaks, as is his custom, only enough words to keep the conversation going:

"I have shown the town to all the distinguished visitors."

"Are there a lot of them?"

"Yes, sir. And very important people. Some years ago, before aviation, I showed the town to the King of France."

"Oh, yes?"

"Yes, sir, just as I am telling you. It was during a trip that he made incognito, strictly incognito. Nobody in the world knew about it!"

Julio Vacas lowers his voice, arches his brows, and speaks in the traveler's ear.

"It was when they elected Don Niceto Alcalá Zamora president. I am going to tell you something that perhaps you don't know, something which has not gotten around much. You will know, but won't say anything, eh?"

"All right."

"Well, he and Don Niceto were cousins."

"Golly!" (IV, 87-88)

Everywhere there are children. Cela, whose own son was
born just a few months before the trip, shows a kindly interest
in them: he talks to the little newspaper boy in Guadalajara,
to the paralytic on the balcony, to the epileptic boy who asks
him for a cigarette, or to the groups of children he meets wherever he goes. Then, there is the little red-haired boy who asks
politely:

"Will you permit me to accompany you some hundred meters?"
And the traveler, who feels a boundless admiration for children who
speak so precisely, answered him.
"Very well, I'll permit you to accompany me some hundred meters."
(IV, 55)

Cela's summary of his literary approach in his travel books
is that fantasy, the interpretation of villages and people, folklore, etc., are just so much nonsense to keep from getting to
the heart of the matter; the best thing to do is take the bull
by the horns and say, "Here is a house, or a tree, or a dying
dog." The style of the house, the utility of the tree, or the
question of whether vaccination would have prolonged the dog's
life are pedantic details in which other travel books abound
(IV, 511). Only at the end, when in Pastrana, does he momentarily lapse from this studied detachment to editorialize over
the pity that provincial monuments are neglected or, worse,
like the tapestries of the former church, shipped off to Madrid
(IV, 231-33).

Yet nostalgia for the glorious old days is at a minimum.
Cela's concern is with the people of the present. In a strict
sense, he has no adventures and is wise enough not to try to
invent them. The worst thing that happens to him is in the
corral of an inn where he is washing after an overcrowded bus
ride with numerous gypsies—one of the best chapters in the
book.

. . . As the traveler bends over, splashing some water on the nape of
his neck, one of the geese gives him such a peck on his hindquarters
that a piece of flesh is not torn away only because the goose misjudged
the distance and struck against a bone.[3] (IV, 222)

II *Across Northern Spain*

In the summer of 1948, Cela is commissioned by the Madrid daily *Pueblo* to make a month's swing around the Spanish peninsula to report on conditions in the vacation hostels for workers established by the government. This excursion by car is really a combined reportorial assignment and inspection tour. The first thirteen of the reports on the northern regions of Galicia, Asturias, Castile, and the Basque Provinces provide the basic raw material for *Del Miño al Bidasoa* (1952). The two rivers of the title lie at opposite ends of the area covered, the first in Galicia and the second on the border between Spain and France.

Contrary to his usual practice, he must travel by automobile —an important detail since it explains an underlying difference between this book and the *Viaje a la Alcarria*. This information, now available in Volume IV of the complete works (247-48, 540), is important for understanding the variation in outlook. In *Del Miño al Bidasoa* he calls himself "vagabond" and attempts to maintain the fiction of the itinerant wanderer. In recasting the articles that appeared first in *Pueblo*, he omits all references to the *paradores* or hostels and the automobile, and at first succeeds in giving the impression that he is the old, impecunious hiker of two years before as he and his companion Dupont hitch a ride on a truck. But we do not very often see him on the open road nor feel the highway beneath his feet; most of the walking takes place on sightseeing tours around various towns. During his rather leisurely itinerary through his native Galicia, the mountains, towns, rivers, and other geographical features simply fly by. No hiker could walk across four provinces in a reasonable time, and if he could, the detailed account of his progress would be impossibly tedious. In the ten days he trudged across the Alcarria he wrote sketches penetrating enough to make the reader share his feelings for the land and its people. But here in *Del Miño al Bidasoa*, something of his problem with *La Catira* arises, though in less objectionable form, as he attempts to digest too much geography.

The material at the beginning is handled with care, but later, although interesting, it becomes a little thin. So, when he speaks

of a religious pilgrimage in the countryside of Pontevedra or
his observations in and around the Santiago de Compostela of
Spain's patron saint, unintentional repetition mars his otherwise
effective presentation; for instance, the "orballo" of Santiago is
mentioned three times in a few pages (IV, 257, 261, 267). Anyone who has ever spent a whole day tramping the streets of
the old cathedral town in the mist-like rain—wearing a summer
suit and, oddly enough, not getting soaked—knows precisely
what Cela means when he says:

> The vagabond, reasonably enough, wants to collect in Compostela
> his abundant supply of water, he wants to fill to the brim the water
> jars of the soul, the same vessels which the sun will relentlessly dry
> up as soon as he returns to traverse the heroic, cruel mesa. (IV, 261)

Just as Cervantes must have discovered soon after Don Quijote's first sortie that a squire like Sancho Panza would greatly
broaden the scope of his novel, so Cela begins to realize that
narrative possibilities with himself as sole protagonist are be-
coming somewhat limited.[4] He then introduces Dupont, the
itinerant seller of toy windmills, in an easy, natural manner
when the peddler approaches and inquires whether he remembers him and his balancing act. Since a fall from the wire had
left him crippled, he has had to take up a more modest but
safer business (IV, 306-8). There is no further physical description of Dupont, but as they travel along together, he becomes
the author's alter ego to such an extent that he even talks and
thinks like him. Further comparison between the itinerant
Frenchman and Don Quijote's companion would be unfair because Cela does not want to develop a striking character who
could possibly turn the travel book into a novel.

Unlike arid, impoverished regions of Castile, the northern
provinces are green, well-watered, and relatively fertile. The
two travelers have no difficulty finding food—supposedly from
handouts—since Dupont has exhausted his stock of windmills.
The reader is incredulous that this manna which sustains them
". . . always comes to hand miraculously . . ." (IV, 410) and
that the author devotes space to gastronomic pleasures. In his

book on the Alcarria food is as hard for him to get as it is for the impoverished people of the region.

The two pass through some of the favorite vacation spots in northern Spain, where the climate is tempered by rainfall and ocean and mountain breezes. In their pose as truly impecunious vagabonds, they keep aloof from the numerous tourists. He feels that Santander, one of the preferred summer resorts, is too rich. His message for those readers of the popular daily *Pueblo*, who feel concern for the economic plight of the more backward regions, has a certain reactionary tone:

Santander is a rare and rich land for the archaeologist and genealogist, for the anthropologist and sociologist, for the agriculturist and industrialist, and even for the antiquarian, the tourist and summer vacationist. If Santander, the green and civilized land of Santander, has too much of anything, it would be possibilities for development.

The vagabond, who habitually prefers the mule to the tractor, and the highway Civil Guard to the scientific and secret police, does not feel too pleased by these fields of Santander before him. (IV, 351)

Although technically Old Castile's outlet to the sea, this thriving city is not a spiritual part of the province (V, 123).

It is not surprising, then, that he is even less enthusiastic about Bilbao, the great industrial city of the Basque Provinces. Industry really is indefensible, he finds, but it must be tolerated because it is useful to others: "The vagabond, if he had to choose between living more calmly and less comfortably without industry, or less uncomfortably and more agitated with it, would prefer the former" (IV, 430), and several pages later he is relieved to find that there remain places in the region which "still live in the peaceful and beautiful times of the pastoral life and of agriculture" (IV, 444). Earlier, however, such scenes recall to him "the bucolic and conservative specters, the shades and spirits of the characters of Pereda of the old and orthodox novel of customs" (IV, 407). The apparent inconsistency results from Cela's realization that literature cannot stay the same as it was in the nineteenth century, but he cannot escape a certain nostalgia for the past which the presence of modern industrial life makes all the more acute.

In addition, there are numerous anecdotes, stories of and encounters with interesting persons, some real and some eccentric and invented. Finally the two travelers pay a visit to Ricardo, the brother of Pío Baroja, in Vera del Bidasoa, and then Dupont bids his friend farewell to return to France. The book ends on a sentimental note as Dupont is lost to view going down a slope of the road, and the author remains surrounded by the minutiae of nature—five ants carrying off a dead wasp ". . . suddenly grown old, though he had not realized it, in the middle of the afternoon, with the sun still swinging high in the sky" (IV, 498).

III *Back in Old Castile*

If Cela's treatment of the northern provinces is at times perfunctory, in *Judíos, moros y cristianos* (1956) he lavishes affectionate attention on an itinerary which forms a rough circle starting at the Navacerrada pass near Madrid, continuing for a hundred miles north to the valley of the Duero and some sixty miles northwest along that river, then turning south to Segovia and thence to Avila, after hitching a ride through the regions of Medina del Campo and Olmedo, to conclude in the Gredos Mountains and his home-base of Cebreros, with an interesting side excursion to the prehistoric site of the stone bulls, so-called, of Guisando.

In his latest prologue, 1963, Cela notes that a careful examination of this book which brought him to the Spanish Academy will reveal a very academic work, a term not to be understood in a pejorative sense (V, 118). Its uncontroversial nature doubtless advanced the author's aspirations. The volume has a great deal of the guidebook about it, being similar to his earlier, pleasant little *Avila* (1952), of the type printed in various languages and sold to tourists in the bookstores and periodical kiosks. At his home in Majorca, Cela has brought together, at his leisure, quite a bit of erudition to add to his presentation— sometimes in imaginary conversations, as, for example, in his talk with an old beggar at the bridge of Roa, who narrates the whole history of the town (V, 186-97). He makes of the beggar the sort of person habitually found on his rambles:

Seated on a pile of gravel for the road, Don Toribio de Mongrovejo de Ortiz de la Seca y de Castilmimbre de Fuentespreadas y de López de Valdeavellano, patient, ancient, and proud as a hawk, was delousing himself. (V, 197)

Previously the beggar has pointed out to the narrator that in the Royal Chancery of Valladolid only the mendicants among practitioners of menial trades such as locksmiths, farriers, clothshearers ever received patents of nobility "because the beggar serves no man, not even the king; he asks in God's name, making it possible for Christians to contribute to the salvation of their souls by performing charitable acts" (V, 197). His words speak volumes about the Spanish religious spirit and the dignity of the individual that Galdós in the past century portrayed so well in *Misericordia*, his novel about beggars.

One cannot doubt the sincerity of Cela's declaration in his latest prologue that he wrote *Judíos, moros y cristianos* as a labor of love (V, 118). He includes at the beginning an earlier, lengthy, and learned prologue on various geographical concepts about the provinces which make up the kingdom of Old Castile; the enumeration of all the toponyms which conserve the Roman designation "Castrum" (Camp), such as Castrojeriz, Castrillo de Duero, etc. (V, 199-201), give evidence of extensive research. More interested in the people than in Segovia's many monuments, he echoes with great feeling the words of Antonio Machado:

In these old cities of Castile, weighted down by tradition, with a Gothic cathedral and twenty Romanesque churches, where one can hardly find a corner without a legend, or a house without its heraldic shield, the eternally beautiful notwithstanding, oh poets and brothers of mine!, is the living present, that which is not written nor ever will be written on stone, from the children playing in the streets—doubly children because they are of the people—and the swallows which fly around the towers, even to the grass of the squares and moss on the roofs. (V, 272)

As early as 1944 [5] Cela expresses the debt of the younger generation to Machado, whom he cites prominently at the begin-

ning of his account of the trip to the Alcarria (IV, 38-39). It is
Machado's concern for humanity, rather than his introspective,
pantheistic spirit, that appeals most to Cela, who implies that
from him he has acquired a compassionate, unpedantic outlook
toward people.[6] This "Poet of the Generation of '98," a symbol
of integrity and resistance—at least subconsciously—to the novelist, died in exile in a concentration camp in southern France
after the defeat of the Republic in 1939. The vagabond's visit
—really a pilgrimage—to the poet's modest lodgings in Segovia,
where he earned his living as an impoverished teacher for thirteen years, is particularly moving (V, 277-79). Spain's leading
serious dramatist, Buero Vallejo, remarked some years ago that
one must know well the works of the truculent Cela to be able
to appreciate his compassion for people.[7]

There is no lack of data and anecdotes about Segovia in this
work, but only two short paragraphs about the cathedral (V,
285-86). His guidebook on Ávila has provided an abundance of
such information (V, 76-81), but he now confesses to no great
enthusiasm for cathedrals in spite of Renan's affirmation that
only those lacking imagination could view them with indifference. Cathedrals appearing somehow unreal, like the theater of
Calderón (V, 357), he prefers less pretentious monuments like
Avila's little church of San Isidro, that has since been moved
to the Retiro Park in Madrid and is apparently destined for
University City. Cela feels a deep sympathy for uprooted monuments.[8] His failure to express indignation at the transformation
of the old Romanesque convent in Ávila into a garage and
filling station is evidently an oversight. Fortunately this building has since been reclaimed for a proposed music conservatory.

When in Madrigal de las Altas Torres, "too much name for
so little town," he engages a local character in conversation as
a means of presenting a quantity of historical information. The
old man, who reminds Cela of a statement heard in medical
school—flies on the trousers' flap are a sign of diabetes—interrupts with impertinent questions and becomes angry at his
refusal to answer; and the narrator can hardly restrain himself
from giving the old man a kick in the place where the flies are
congregated (V, 325-27). Another form of the same contrapuntal

technique is later used to narrate the life of Santa Teresa, where, after greeting the bootblack Merejo in the square named for the saint, he presents a lengthy paragraph about him, two lines on Santa Teresa, another section on Merejo, two more lines on the saint, alternating thus for several pages (V, 350-53).

Since this narration is an anecdote about the painful but ludicrous mishap of the bootblack as a sometime bullfighter, the reader may feel that Cela is perhaps being irreverent. On the contrary, he is trying to show the two polarities of Spanish life, one rooted in earthiness, the other in mysticism. Nor is he given to nostalgia for old ruins; his sympathy is for those living and suffering in the present. Calling Madrigal "a ruined ballad," he remains untouched by the fact that at one time its walls and towers, if not as grandiose as those of Ávila, were at least impressive. On my visit to Madrigal, I noted the gates, towers, and walls lying in heaps and heard one resident's apt summary of the situation: "We live here amidst ruins."

The three races of the title *Judíos, moros y cristianos* are suggested to him probably by the writings of Américo Castro, who has stressed repeatedly the symbiosis of these three peoples in the development of Spanish culture. Cela, however, does not attempt to any extent a synthesis of ethnic relations. He recounts a few local legendary miracles about Jews and the Host, a Jew's attempt to mock some Christian martyrs (V, 275-76, 359), and the old story of the ritual murder of a child —the Santo Niño de la Guardia—in 1489, which in part provoked the disorders leading to the expulsion of the Jews in 1492 (V, 348-49). Anticipating his new role of academician, he is not averse to being linked eruditely with Américo Castro, but the title of the book is a little misleading.[9] In all fairness to Cela, it must be said that he reiterates his opposition to prejudice by dismissing the fifteenth-century evangelist San Vicente Ferrer as a racist who made the Moors wear green-hooded cloaks with silver moons, and the Jews tabards with blood-red insignia. The absurdity of racial prejudice is revealed in rather fanciful imagery about the children playing in the square, some wearing "a bright moon painted on the green cloaks with which they cover their heads . . . and backs of their souls," others

"displaying a red mark on the tabard with which they clothe
their wills" (V, 162-63). This tender scene recalls Machado's
words: "The eternally beautiful . . . is the living present . . .
the children playing in the streets."

IV *First Andalusian Trip*

Part of the tour of workers' vacation resorts in the summer
of 1948 takes Cela to Andalusia. His notes of the excursion with
additional material (IV, 247-48) form the basis of *Primer viaje
andaluz* (1959). Although some of the information appeared in
newspapers, the later travel notes do not appear in book form
until a considerable time has elapsed. This interim he evidently
devotes to a search for details that will give more perspective
to his originally journalistic approach. *Primer viaje andaluz,*
therefore, portrays a traveler reluctant to leave Castile and the
northern provinces for the considerably more colorful, picturesque (these commonplace adjectives one uses deliberately)
southern region, long the favorite mecca for tourists with romantic, stereotyped ideas about Spain. The region (or regions, for
there are several in Andalusia) has received memorable treatment from serious folklorists and writers on customs, as well as
from poets of the sixteenth century to modern writers such as
García Lorca and Juan Ramón Jiménez, to mention only the
most distinguished. Can Cela apply his own technique to this
varied geography and culture and say something new?

It is an exaggeration to say that, with his academic, popular,
and financial successes, Cela has lost some of his zest for the
road,[10] but he himself remarks in the prologue to this fourth
book of travels that, even though he has additional notes on
numerous other regions, "the vagabond is tired; . . . and wouldn't
be surprised . . . to put a final period to this chapter of his
vagabondage, already lengthy in scope. It will be a sad day
for him." [11] It will indeed, for some of his finest pages have
caught the homely scenes and people of the Spanish countryside, now starting to change rapidly under the impact of the
technical and economic revolution of the last twenty-five years.
Cela will be for the twenty-first century what Larra, Mesonero,
and Estébanez Calderón are for this—a writer who captures

the customs of his country on the eve of change. He continues to collect his earlier sketches and travel impressions, most recently in *Páginas de geografía errabunda* (*Pages of Wandering Geography*), 1965, which include notes assembled for a *Segundo viaje andaluz*, (*Second Andalusian Trip*), subtitled significantly *A Book That Was Never Written*.[12]

So, in the account of his first Andalusian tour, Cela reminds us that he bade farewell to Dupont at the end of *Del Miño al Bidasoa*. He will not knight his companion as Don Quijote was honored (27) because he has deserted the trip (the writer asks forgiveness for using this harsh term). Despeñaperros Pass, the abrupt gorge that is New Castile's gateway to Andalusia, lies halfway across Spain, and he shows himself in no hurry to arrive there. A third of the book passes, and he has not yet entered the region. "The South frightens the vagabond . . . a man of other latitudes, . . . different scenes, . . . dawns and sunsets . . . . [It] . . . is the remote and indecipherable land of the 'piripao'" (77-78). He perhaps exaggerates his own regional affinities, a typically Spanish trait, but there is no denying the emotion that entering a new district arouses in him; he later finds the province of Cordova as strange as an Englishman would (208).

He has earlier reemphasized his dislike of large cities (182); there is no doubt that he feels more at home in the open country and small towns. His problem is accentuated on this trip by the fact that such monumental cities as Cordova and Seville have been so often written about that it is difficult to be original. Yet he manages to fill a sizable volume, 382 pages in the edition available, not including the two indices of personal and place names. The itinerary is generally in a southwesterly direction through Cordova to Seville and on to the Portuguese border. Cela provides a variety of tidbits along the way, such as a reference to the school for bullfighters in Alcalá de Guadaira run by Sidney Franklin, formerly of Brooklyn, and to the skilled pastry cook in Castilleja de la Cuesta who is Rita Hayworth's grandfather (246, 328).

Contrary to his principles, the vagabond must enter the Andalusian cities. Eventually we find him enumerating the various

points of interest in Cordova, taking the occasion to point out
that no writer—not even Juan Valera, who was practically a
native, or Baroja, one of whose novels takes place there—has
ever captured the real atmosphere of the Plaza del Mercado
(193). At length, Cela and an acquaintance go off to spend the
evening listening to flamenco music (194-96).

His problem of finding something original to report is even
greater in Seville. He repeats his dislike of imposing monuments (184) and museums; he has disliked such institutions
ever since he was kicked out of the National Library in Madrid,
not for stealing books, but for wanting to read them (262). That
incident may explain why he takes pains to quote the statement
of a former director of the library who said in an interview
that he knew nothing of contemporary literature since he had
no time to read (I, 28-29). Cela himself by contrast possesses
a broad knowledge of Spanish literature which serves as docu-
mentation for his works; thus, when he is confronted by the
Giralda of the Cathedral of Seville, he cites verses from five
poets, beginning with Lope de Vega in the seventeenth century
and ending with Fernando Villalón in the twentieth, recalling
in the process a little passage from *Don Quijote* (272-74).

Cela's great talent has always been the ability to invent
fascinating types or to make memorable the real persons he
encounters; unfortunately their number in the later travel books
is rather small. With a certain nostalgia, then, he meets Martín
of *Viaje a la Alcarria*, the former bicycle-riding peddler of
hempen sandals, who now travels on a Vespa and sells radios,
chemical fertilizers, water pumps, repair parts for motorcycles
and automobiles, and farm machinery (241-42), and rides into
Seville with him. He varies the account of his sightseeing by
introducing the flamenco-singing Garrobo sisters. One of them
accompanies him on an orgy in the Triana quarter lasting several days—the time element is left conveniently vague. Here
the vagabond has the opportunity to expatiate on types of
flamenco songs (295-321).

V A Trip to the Pyrenees

Cela's most recent travel book, *Viaje al Pirineo de Lérida*

(*Trip to the Pyrenees of Lérida*), 1965,[13] possibly the last tour of this type, is probably not much inferior to the two preceding. While the others describe colorful, well-known places whether the author felt up to expounding about them or not, this itinerary covers a very circumscribed mountain region in the Pyrenees just south and west of Andorra. He writes the prologue seven years after the 1956 excursion. There is no doubt that the scenery he describes and illustrates with numerous photographs is some of the most striking in Europe. The author's picture on the cover, reclining by a stream and displaying a certain middle-aged corpulence, makes it seem all the more likely that he will soon be leaving the open road for good.

As one reads and rereads certain works, he becomes conscious of repeated formulas, personal quirks, recurrence of favorite words, which can become a little annoying after a time; but such careful study also brings an awareness of both good and bad qualities. In *Viaje al Pirineo* Cela seems to be going through an established routine. Whereas in *Viaje a la Alcarria* he states that the book is geography without the usual encyclopedic detail, in the later volumes there is no lack of such academic information—perhaps the result of his rather self-conscious status as a member of the Spanish Academy. So, there are itineraries in guidebook style, including three imaginary ones in case the reader may be interested; just to contemplate the climb involved in one of them leaves Cela with tongue hanging out (164-69, 172-76, 189-92). He enters into a discussion of place names, their etymologies and orthography, even including footnotes; and while these items are not unimportant, they become rather involved—for instance, he relates Arán with, among other things, "arándano" or cranberry (148-49).

His description of eating places reads at times like the *Guide Michelin*, and once he even uses the terms "three stars" and "four stars," with recipes and, practically dropping the pretense of the impecunious vagabond, an enumeration of the various courses at meals. He recounts local legends, lists places, rivers, and mountains, and expresses his pet peeves against the encroachment of progress on the old landmarks or the removal of church paintings and murals to the museum in Barcelona.

A new vexation is the creation of national parks in the area, together with the installations contained therein.

Cela frequently exhibits a fascination with the regional plants and flowers which he, as a collector, feels make good souvenirs; he has little patience with the usual mementos sought by tourists:

The traveler personally feels that to exchange one's memory, that noble and personal sentiment, for what is offered to spare us the pleasant effort of recollection, is an error as serious and miserable as that of confusing frequent visits to a brothel with love. . . . Few tourists think of taking away a real souvenir (all the worse for them!) . . . such as God provides every morning and offers to any who want it: a twig, a sprig of fern, the fuzzy and rustic petal, blood-red or shining like gold. (198)

There is little doubt that Cela is enjoying himself in this region of no large cities, but he deplores the inevitable hordes of tourists drawn by the area's proximity to France and pleasant summer resorts like Espot:

. . . a very civilized town and attractive to excursionists, with young ladies of large posteriors in trousers, young people listening to radios and drinking vermouth, gentlemen in shirtsleeves and suspenders, fat ladies dressed in cretonne, with wicked intentions shining in their eyes and timid moustaches adorning their powdered upper lips. There are women who should be prohibited by law. (108)

It would be possible to return Espot to its original state, as noble as any in the Pyrenees—"perhaps it would be enough to wash its face of the artificial city dirt which stains it."

Whatever shortcomings these recent travel books may exhibit, there is no loss of self-expression—he even uses explicit terms to describe the act of defecation (48). But then, again, there is the humorous, touching scene of his encounter with the nondescript dog that will become his companion. He tries to select a suitable name for it. When he finally calls him Llir, the old and poetic form of the Catalan for lily, "the little mutt began to jump and bound so enthusiastically that the traveler understood clearly that if that wasn't his name, it was indeed what he wanted always to be called" (138). Later, in his description of the dog's death under the wheels of a truck, he hides his sentimentality under the deceptive stylistic baldness affected by some contemporary writers (265-67).

Cela, like many thoughtful Spaniards, cannot view economic progress and the influx of tourists—even though these things bring money and create jobs—without mixed feelings. In one town a swarm of French travelers is having an outing, probably some sort of religious pilgrimage since priests and nuns are in attendance. The festivities are occasionally punctuated with cries of "Viva España!" A nun gives him a piece of bread, and Cela grumbles:

"Your charity is appreciated, sister, may God repay you. Long live Spain! Wouldn't you like to take my picture? I can put on either the expression of a native of an underdeveloped country . . . or that of one eternally grateful; you have a choice." (246)

The author of course has notes on other regions of Spain. One can only speculate about their later appearance in book form. If Ediciones Alfaguara, in which Cela has a financial interest, finds them profitable, in all probability they will be forthcoming—like the seventy-nine-page profusely illustrated *Madrid* (1966) for which Spanish booksellers charge $6.00. The little volume may provide a souvenir for tourists, or the brief notes on places and sights—hardly more than a paragraph long in most cases—may prove useful to them. There are four pages on bullrings with several bland watercolor illustrations reminiscent of those in children's books; the information about the Royal Spanish Academy and its members is of interest to Hispanists, but there are only nine lines of text in two pages on the Royal Palace, and that, as the author admits, cannot do it justice. This type of publication is one aspect of the new directions in Cela's literary output.

CHAPTER 10

Current Tendencies

WHILE Cela has not written another novel to receive wide attention since *La colmena,* if one disregards the controversial *La Catira,* his books roll off the presses with such rapidity that it is difficult for a critic on this side of the Atlantic to keep track of them. His remarks in prologues to new works and additional prefaces to earlier ones can never be ignored, but some care in interpretation is essential, although Cela is as honest about his writings as many other authors, and no more prone to make literature of his experiences than they. The new introductions, however, are written after the fact for books first published some ten or fifteen years before, and they are thus a reply to critical judgments motivated by various prejudices—especially by the rigid concept of what a novel should or should not be. *La familia de Pascual Duarte* and *La colmena* continue to influence contemporary Spanish writers, but certain innovations in his other works may not gain rapid acceptance. An analogy with his writings may be seen in the original *Lazarillo de Tormes,* which became an instant success in the middle of the sixteenth century in spite of being placed on the Index, but its implications were not assimilated by Mateo Alemán in *Guzmán de Alfarache* until 1599.[1]

I *The Protean Genre*

The novel has always been hard to define. Examination of conventional definitions in manuals and dictionaries in the light of practice soon reveals discrepancies because many diverse books are called novelistic for want of a better term. In the

140

prologue to his only recent novel, *Tobogán de hambrientos* (*Toboggan of Hungry People*), 1962,[2] Cela summarizes a common definition of the genre as ". . . everything which exceeds the length of the tale and the short novel and is written in narrative prose . . . ," but it is no less puerile to try to give the novel norms it cannot follow (12). Elsewhere, he claims to have gathered together over 300 definitions,[3] but his own varied novelistic structure prevents a clear determination of personal preferences. He seems to shun the long classical, epical narration as cultivated by Gironella in the protracted account (921 pages) of the vicissitudes of the Alvear family during the Civil War years in *Los cipreses creen en Dios* (*The Cypresses Believe in God*) and in his sequels. When Cela writes of individual protagonists as in *Timoteo el incomprendido* (*Misunderstood Timothy*), he limits himself to the novelette, and seems deliberately to avoid involvement with his characters or, possibly, even loses interest in them.

The novel must have a skeleton, he says, using analogies with favorite animals. Earlier he compares the tale to a pony and the novel to a Percheron (III, 491). A novel like the *Lazarillo* has the skeleton of a rabbit and *The Magic Mountain* that of an elephant with appropriate flesh (13), while *Tobogán* has the skeleton of a snake because in this life everything is a concatenation with no unattached pieces (14).

The narrative of *Tobogán de hambrientos* is circular so that after the first hundred vignettes one begins a return to the starting point and reaches it after the two hundredth, with the character of the first sketch killing himself when his mother dies—thus ending the series of stories and breaking the symmetry of the circle. After his futile attempts to make a living by telling fortunes with cards—usually a feminine profession—the pathetic man commits suicide, an act which has abnormal implications. The final lines are more for effect than anything else:

After several days, Florencio Basilio Pérez appeared floating on the unhealthy and turgid waters of the Manzanares, with his eyes open, his belly swollen, and in his pocket a portrait of his mother dressed as a bride and smiling, rather cheerfully, at the world. (457)

One is inclined to discount somewhat Cela's pronouncements
when he realizes that they serve a structural purpose in the
book itself—that is, to make the artifice more plausible and
palatable. In fact, the straight-faced prologue is quite in keeping with his personality. Basically he rearranges the little
sketches or chapters or episodes by using a varied procedure,
but the essential material resembles that of the *Apuntes carpetovetónicos* which, he says in Volume III of the *Obra completa* (28), attain their most mature form in *Tobogán*. The
passages are amusing, at times even touching, and reflect a lack
of stiffness of treatment, greater facility, more polished humor,
without the "tough fiber" of the *Apuntes*. Besides his gift of
observation, Cela has a talent for caricature that predominates
over the portrayal of reality and results in an imbalance—for
some readers—in much of his recent writing.

Various passages are a fairly accurate statement of his ideas.
Thus, in *Tobogán* he makes fun of the lady physical culture
expert called Punching-ball, who has written a "tremendista"
novel that, under different titles, has been runner-up in several
literary competitions. In her book the hero pardons the heroine's
infidelity, and—after several improbable adventures—both are
killed in a plane crash in the Persian Gulf (48-49). Or there
is the refined young man who is collecting pretty thoughts for
a proposed book *Florecillas de mi sendero* (*Little Flowers on
My Path*), 102-4. Then again, a young author in the café drinks
and smokes constantly and eats anything that comes along, but
writes

. . . obsessively, with application, inexorably, as though he were ill,
as though his life depended on placing the last period, to be able to
breathe, almost sadly, with pride and stupefaction. With all due al-
lowances, in this way *Crime and Punishment*, for example, was
written, or *The Brothers Karamazov*, or *Anna Karenina*, . . . three
admirable novels. (273)

Here Cela has expressed his contempt for or approval of three
approaches to literary craftsmanship. In the first series of *Los
viejos amigos* (1960, 82-84), he develops further a theme presented in the novelette *Café de artistas* (1953) about the poor

wretch who tries to follow the precept that the novel has three
elements, expounded by a pompous editor:

"Well, they are exposition, crisis, and denouement. Without exposition, crisis, and denouement, no matter how you want to look at it,
there is no novel; what there is, do you want me to tell you?"
"Yes, sir, yes indeed."
"Well, for your information, there is nothing. What there is is
deceit and modernism!"
Poor Cirilo was overwhelmed, dazed. The editor used very solid
arguments.

One could argue endlessly about the proper classification of
Tobogán and not reach a conclusion. Those who insist that the
novel should follow a conventional pattern leave no more room
for innovation than those who would insist that the theater
should purvey only drama in the tradition of the well-made play.
Though the main concern here is pointing out new tendencies
in Cela's work, certain comparisons between this and his earlier
writings suggest themselves. The division of *Tobogán* into two
parts composed of essentially parallel elements, with individuals
appearing and reappearing for approximately the same amount
of space, recalls the technique of *Pabellón de reposo*, but with
a larger cast. This treatment of such large numbers reminds us
of *La colmena*, which did not depart so much from the conventional novel of many characters, except that their presentation
is momentary and there is no central protagonist save the anti-
hero Martín Marco. In *Tobogán* Cela develops the process
further by proceeding from person to person as their relationships—acquaintance, friend, sweetheart, parent, relative—lead
from one to the other. Sometimes the association is almost
mechanically offered to introduce the next individual in the
sequence.
    Not that the persons—"infraheros" one reviewer calls them [4]
—lack interest; they are amusing and at times even moving;
and Cela has definite theories about them.[5] The title—a toboggan filled with hungry people—portrays well the idea of men
and women on the skids, seldom succeeding, who hunger for
something lacking in their lives, although human misery—no

longer presented as a scrounging for food and sex as in *La colmena*—is submerged under their personal idiosyncrasies with considerable attenuation of dramatic tensions. The critic writing in Cela's own *Papeles* suggests that the author has depicted photographically "the elements of a society . . . as a case to be remedied; he does not make fun of it, and if he presents its defects, it is because they obsess him . . . ." [6] This nod to the sociological novel is unconvincing. If Cela does anything for certain types of humble Spanish people, it is to make them a part of literature, thereby compensating for their traditionally inarticulate roles in society.

There are other changes in technique. In the travel books he often breaks up his presentation with conversation, sometimes even resorting to talking to himself. Since dialogue has always been one of his strong points, Cela does well to utilize it in any way possible. Therefore, without trite preliminaries, in *Tobogán* he simply breaks into the narration, even speaking with the reader:

Carlotita's mother-in-law is named Felipa and she dyes her hair a mandarin-orange color.

"You already said that."

"Yes, I know, but now it seems a good idea to repeat it."

"Well, never mind; don't let me stop you. That would be the last straw." (99)

At other times Cela speaks to another party as though two persons were gossiping about a third.

Pelagio Cabezuela Rebollo, Míster Pipermín in the bullring, but outside of the ring, Caca, if you will pardon the expression, because of the odor.

"What if he took a bath?"

"Don't even think of it, man, don't even think of it! Do you want to ruin him? His life is at stake! Pelagio says the odor is his defense, because when the bull gets close and smells him, it runs away."

"Ah! Well, in that case, I have nothing to say. That is an instinct for self-preservation."

"Of course, man, of course, probably!"

However, Pelagio's body is covered with scars, evidently from gorings by bulls who have a bad sense of smell. (113)

The use of such laconic humor is frequent in *Tobogán*, and his deft touch with a wide gamut of sentimental nuances makes him a master of portraying subtle human relationships. The tenderness of his description of the paralytic girl "beautiful and sad like the lonely flower of the moor" (154) strikes us as all the more sincere when we recall his fondness for wild flowers. The frequent visits of Julito, a young gentleman and neighbor, are Esther's only pleasure. Her father invites him to go some place where they can talk, insists on paying for drinks and supper, and guzzles vermouth.

. . . At one thirty, Don Fernando kissed Julito on the forehead.
"If you think I am drunk, you are mistaken. The fact is that I am very fond of you, Julito, and I am very grateful. . . . You, don't let anyone see you . . . take these twenty duros and tomorrow morning, without anyone knowing, buy some flowers for Esther . . . ."
Don Fernando began to cry.
"Don't pay any attention to me, Julito, you can see I am drunk . . . ." (157)

In Part II nothing has changed with Esther and Julito. She asks him, as usual, if he has a girlfriend, someone to take for a walk, to invite to a café, to take to the movies or dancing. And Julito responds:

"The important thing is to love her . . . , although she cannot leave the house . . . ."
Tears filled Esther's eyes.
"What did you say?"
"Nothing, Esther, I didn't say anything. . . . I was talking to myself . . . ." (321)

But what happens if the reader becomes interested in the lives of such persons? Leaving aside all discussion about what constitutes a novel, he is bound to feel frustration when he is forced to go on to other characters who may or may not interest him particularly. It is possible that Cela himself has had similar feelings, for in the two series of *Los viejos amigos* (1960, 1961)[7] he revisits certain ones who have appeared in earlier works. It is a commonplace to say that fictional characters come to have an independent existence, and so in the prologue to this series he qualifies this thought: "The author begets and gives birth, in due time, to his characters—that is certain—but his characters are not his own . . ." (I, 9), although he adds that they do not belong to humanity, to literary history, to the public domain, but to themselves (I, 10).

It is quite possible that Cela has thought of reviving some of his protagonists, because in his travel books he met real people whom he incorporated into the narrative. Even if they are imaginary, he claims to receive news about them from time to time. If this is a literary artifice, it is a good one. Now in *Los viejos amigos* one is intrigued by the fact that each volume of the series contains seven chapters further developing characters named in *La colmena*, a process all the more fascinating when it is noticed that the chapters fall at almost identical places in the two volumes (I, 49, 93, 138, 178, 221, 263, 302; II, 49, 91, 135, 180, 222, 264, 305). Likewise, further examination shows that other earlier works are utilized systematically throughout the two volumes so that by following the pattern of Series I one can usually predict which will provide the material for the next selection in Series II. Cela's orderly mind is evident. His books have a balanced structure even when it is hardly needed. And we learn thus, something of his methods of composition for the later volumes. He keeps systematic files of his manuscripts and stories published in periodicals. Nothing is discarded. It seems likely, then, that Cela is resurrecting material omitted from *La colmena* in its various revisions. The novel was characterized by a kaleidoscopic, unifying grim view throughout, composed of carefully assembled bits, less than a page in length. In *Los viejos amigos* the chapters are two or three pages long, and their tone is generally more humorous, more indulgent, than that of *La colmena*. He must have regretted having to excise them, but the excision is so skillfully done that *La colmena* always moves without dragging. In any case, the omitted selections appear in *Los viejos amigos*, disclosing a more tolerant view of society.

II *Pictorial Storytelling*

In 1962, 1963, and 1964 Cela published six more books, easily divisible into three groups. The first is composed of two lengthy volumes of miscellaneous stories and sketches of a type with which we are already familiar: *Las compañías convenientes y otros fingimientos y cegueras* (*Suitable Companions and Other Deceits and Obfuscations*), a work which includes many tales reprinted from earlier collections; and *Garito de hospicianos o guirigay de imposturas y bambollas* (*Poorhouse Inmates or Jargon of Frauds and Shams*), a number of editorializing essays inspired by short news items which, because of their human interest and humor, are used as column fillers. The second group is composed of three profusely illustrated little books, often with one page of text for each illustration, as in *Gavilla de fábulas sin amor, Once cuentos de fútbol con once pinturas de Pepe,* and *El solitario*. With its highly imaginative prose, this second group represents at least a new type of packaging that is characteristic of Cela's most recent production. Finally there are the two small volumes with realistic texts and black-and-white photographs entitled *Toreo de salón* and *Izas, rabizas y colipoterras*.

In none of these works is there anything which can really be called a novel; at best, in some of the shorter ones the novelette is all that is discernible. It seems rather pointless, therefore, to discuss whether or not *Garito de hospicianos* is a novel, as a recent critic has done.[8] In his prologue Cela drops his usual defense of the amorphous novel and speaks simply of literature:

The day will come when a courageous writer will decide to take the sane course and set fire to everything which today is torturing literature. . . .

But let us not indulge in the vain accounts of the milkmaid—that also is literature—because it is possible that dreaming, with one's eyes slightly closed, about that triumphant and incendiary date is, if one looks at the matter carefully, only vague and pleasant literature. (13-14)

These last words are quite applicable to the collection as a whole. There is no denying the charm of many of the little compositions inspired by news dispatches from all over the world. Because there are so few of them from Spain, it is hard to see how they can be considered sketches of customs in the traditional Hispanic sense. Cela, as usual, succeeds in extracting their human side—at times with a certain melancholy note— as in the first selection based on a story with dateline Daytona entitled "Lluvia de estrellas" ("Rain of Stars"), about an infinite number of starfish washed up on the beach (17-20). He recalls Sir Malcolm Campbell and the Spanish explorer Cabeza de Vaca, who passed near Daytona, and manages to join these unrelated elements in an ingenious manner—Campbell because of the beach, and Cabeza de Vaca, like the starfish, cast up by the sea. Among the book's illustrations are newspaper clippings about the death of Medgar Evers and a pending visit of Richard Nixon to Europe, which is to include Spain. In fact, the number of items about the United States is considerable.

The most striking of the illustrated books is *Gavilla de fábulas*, (1962) with drawings by Picasso, awarded the Ibarra medal as the best edited work of 1965. Cela has taken each of the thirty-two colored crayon sketches of rather comic faces, for the most part, and provided a text introduced usually with quotations from Spanish poets of the Middle Ages and the sixteenth century. It is perhaps unnecessary to say that the two "Trancos" entitled "Razón de amor" ("An Account of Love") and "La historia troyana" ("The History of Troy") into which the book is divided are not intended to present any sort of connected narrative of the Spanish, universal, exotic, mythical, or heroic themes which Cela has brought together. They deal with erotic and classical material respectively. This variety gives his fantasy free rein to indulge in some of his most daringly scabrous or lyrical language—not entirely new tendencies with him. But in all the works examined to date, including *Pabellón de reposo* and *Mrs. Caldwell habla con su hijo*, the more indelicate passages are rather incidental. Now Cela utilizes an increasingly rich vocabulary, even more marked in other current works, so that many a native Spaniard can consult a dictionary from time to time.

Occasionally *Gavilla* descends to puerilities—for instance, in the selection about medieval ladies in their chastity belts masturbating with the aid of tame rats (35-36); now and then the text seems pretty heavy-handed when compared to the delicacy of the line drawings. The reader is conscious of an effort being made to transcend a style often characterized as "primores de lo vulgar" ("exquisiteness of the ordinary"). And, indeed, Adam and Eve are presented as just another couple. Yet in "El reloj de flora" ("The Clock of Flowers"), Cela lists those blossoms which open at various times of the day for the entire twenty-four hour cycle. The Picasso doves appear, of course, in the chapter "Novela rosa y oro" ("A Pink and Gold Novel") about the courtship of doves. The many references to works of art found in the text add an interesting dimension.

El solitario is a series of texts to accompany the hallucinatory pen-and-ink drawings of Rafael Zabaleta which deliberately imitate the style of old etchings. They are filled with eerie perspectives, a yellowish illumination suggestive of moonlight, nude females, the devil, various winged gargoyle-like creatures, an occasional octopus, graves, fragments of corpses, men and women in Victorian garb seated in overstuffed rooms having a general atmosphere of fin-de-siècle decadence. At the beginning there are allusions to the carnage of World War I and pictures of soldiers with insignia suggestive of this holocaust. The "solitario"—the restless, suffering spirit of a dead soldier roaming the world—is a voyeur contemplating rather weird goings on. *El solitario* and *Gavilla de fábulas* in this "Secret Museum" series are presumably intended for bibliophiles since they were first published in limited folio art editions. It seems to be taken for granted that there is something depraved in the mildly titillating eroticism of these books.

There is a certain monotony to the book, a fault probably of the sketches which do not allow much scope to Cela's fancy. The Picasso volume is far superior in variety and deftness of touch, and in it the author is at least able to produce a tour-de-force. *El solitario* is divided into three sections dedicated to the traditional enemies of the soul—the world, the flesh, and the devil. There are a few unkind remarks about warmongers at

the beginning, but this pacifist note is not sustained. To create
this somnambulistic journey, Cela returns to the dream world—
a recurring device in his works—to deal with his highly personal Weltanschauung.

Once cuentos de fútbol, with their candid color drawings by
eight-year-old Pepe, would seem to have little in common with
the lugubrious vision of *El solitario*, but there is a surprising
similarity of approach. So, for example, he takes the barest
suggestion of a theme related to soccer and embroiders it with
the most incongruous, unrelated material. In the selection about
the agent Don Teopempo Luarca Novillejo—the name is relatively straightforward in comparison with the increasingly bizarre ones of these later works—there are quotations at the
beginning from the *Panchatantra*: an account of Don Teopempo's wanderings; of his Dominican wife, fat, sentimental, and
mulatto, who sings "Carmen" and recites the poetry of the
Mexican Amado Nervo while showing the whites of her eyes;
of the husband's success formula learned from a book by Mr.
Skillet, a senator from Nebraska who died in Spain while working as an extra during the filming of *The Pride and the Passion*;
plus various other disparate elements. The connection of Don
Teopempo, alias Pigeon, with soccer is his importation and ex-
portation of ballplayers whom he prepares for shipment by
embalming, symbolic of the cold indifference of the mercenary
aspect of the sport. Cela's preposterous language recalls the
expressionistic "esperpento" cultivated by Valle-Inclán, the caricature suggesting figures distorted by fun-house mirrors and
sometimes considered an ingredient of "tremendismo." With
Cela, however, the grotesque satire of public figures or deflated
heroes is absent for obvious reasons.[9]

Such exaggerations cause the reader to feel that the whole
thing is a mystification. Cela is clearly poking fun at certain
types of persons connected with football promotion, and character portrayal in the usual sense is non-existent. Quite likely
Cela also has reservations about the football mania of his com-
patriots, because at the end of the book (81) he speaks wryly
of those hundreds of thousands, perhaps millions, of Spanish
fans whose hearts are wrapped up for life in the *Hoja de Lunes*,

the newspaper which carries the results of the Sunday games. His attitude becomes clearer when we realize that earlier in his career his football reportages were suspended because he did not take the game seriously enough.[10]

But there can be no doubt about his personal sympathies in *Toreo de salón,* the first of the current books illustrated with photographs whose grainy quality serves to accentuate their harshness. Here he writes texts in the older, perceptive manner about aspiring young bullfighters who practice their passes at dummy bulls' heads propelled toward them on bicycle wheels. The style is simple, somewhat humorous, a bit repetitive, but understanding in spirit.

It is easier to fight a Miura bull than to fight in the drawing room. People don't think so, but it's true. . . . In real bullfighting . . . the torero comes out, and the bull, if he is a real bull and knows the rules of the game, does the rest. The drawing-room bullfighter has no help. Besides a torero, he must be a great dramatic actor to fight in the drawing room. To say, "Pass bull!" to a chair which remains stationary is much less normal than to say it to a live bull that probably goes by so fast one doesn't even have time to say it. ("Introitus," 1-2)

Izas, rabizas y colipoterras (1964) presents a close-up of the seamy side of Barcelona prostitution, with appropriate photographs and texts about the women involved. The book created something of a sensation in Spain and sold briskly, but there followed the predictable critical opinion that Cela was primarily concerned with shocking the bourgeoisie, a not unlikely possibility. But it is also an unwavering look at one side of life that respectable people try to pretend does not exist; the author is not one to indulge in mawkish sentimentality for people of any social stratum. Anonymous verses from the *Cancionero general,* Antwerp, 1557, quoted at the beginning, provide the title and five general categories into which the prostitutes and the volume are divided. Cela displays a lexicographical dexterity in choosing terms for prostitutes that he resurrects from older Spanish literature, but the sympathy underneath the at times jocose language is lost on the sensation-seeking reader. In the

dedicatory note to my personal copy, Cela speaks with pity
of these "bitter, Hispanic, suffering 'izas'," sentiments repeated
in the work:

Petrita is the political fox of Aristotle, the vixen created to live in
society. Petrita is a peripatetic strumpet, a magpie who shows the
way in her rounds . . . . Ah, Petrita—what a pity the world is out
of joint!—would have made a fine mother of a family.
"The day I win at the football pools I am going back to my town
to be married in church." (60)

. . . .

. . . The "Lizard" keeps in a shoebox fifteen or twenty nude photo-
graphs of herself as a young girl.
. . . The "Lizard" sometimes opens her shoebox and shows the photos
to guests and visitors.
"Is that your daughter?"
"No, I don't have any daughters. That's me when I was young."
"Yes?"
"Yes, me. What's the matter?"
The "Lizard" is accustomed to sun herself at the door; that is a
cheap amusement and doesn't bother anyone. (84)

. . . . . .

Let us not cast blame, because we are all sinners. Let us depart
in silence dragging after us the phantom of our bruised consciences.
Here end the five exercises on the bawds, harlots, hustlers, strumpets,
and tarts. Let him who is without sin cast the first stone at the
woman . . . . (86)

Writing in *Indice* about *La colmena*, Cela reveals a somewhat
naturalistic tendency: "What I wanted to do [was] . . . go out
into the square with my little photographic apparatus . . . .
If my models were ugly, deformed, or undernourished, too
bad! "[11] He uses this same camera technique in the seven series
of *Nuevas escenas matritenses* (1965-1966),[12] copiously illustrated
with photographs from all, particularly the more humble, cor-
ners of Madrid. No doubt he has made inhabitants of the capital
see for the first time persons they pass every day without being
aware of them. His skill with words is undiminished, and the
combined photos and texts have great documentary value in that

they preserve the spirit of a rapidly changing Madrid. In the final series of *Escenas* (21-26), he continues to view Spanish industrialization with a jaundiced eye. Even Cela does not realize, perhaps, the full impact that the automobile will have on urban life; the registration of motor vehicles has already passed the half-million mark in both Madrid and Barcelona. The title of the series calls to mind the *Escenas matritenses* (*Madrid Scenes*) of Mesonero Romanos, who, over a hundred years ago, set down the customs of a city in transition.

Among other illustrated works, he has brought out four volumes in a series *A la pata de palo* (*The Man with the Wooden Leg*) which includes *Historias de España* (*Stories of Spain*), published as a book in 1958, with humorous and grotesque drawings by Goñi; it has the usual striking jacket and contains vignettes about blind men and village idiots. In the last selection of the first part, the author reveals his bitterness at the unfeeling attitude of his countrymen toward the unfortunate. Some blind men using clubs are to fight a bull bedecked with a cowbell; since they too wear the bells, they quite naturally belabor one another. Unluckily this good clean fun is interrupted by the rain, and the public goes off for a glass of wine.

El ciudadano Iscariote Reclús (*Citizen Iscariote Reclús*), 1965, in the same series, is about an eccentric's transmigrations —the metempsychosis which intrigues Cela, however much he may joke about it. The characterizations are similar to those in *Tobogán*. In *Papeles*, No. CXXIX, 1966, he publishes "Cartas a mi querida esposa morganática" ("Letters to my Beloved Morganatic Wife") from an earlier incarnation that reveal something of the fantasy of *Mrs. Caldwell*. The final lines promise more of the same if the former wife makes them available, a suggestion that at least one short work of this type may be forthcoming. Even though Cela provides nothing very new, the element of karma gives a somewhat different slant to the material. His concept of reincarnation, a little unearthly, hardly becomes a leitmotiv of the proportions found in Joyce's *Ulysses*;[13] for both writers it may imply a belief in a sort of eternity in the face of an absurd universe.[14] That the ludicrous and the obscene are mingled in Cela as in Joyce is thought-provoking.

These lines about Reclús' Franciscan love of the birds he domes-
ticates by feeding them bread crumbs exemplify this tendency:

. . . Finally, they even got close enough to shit on him and everything. It was a pleasure to see them with their happy chirping and
springy little bounds. Wild animals want to live and be left in peace.
Not man. What man likes is to irk his neighbor, piss on his geraniums,
and put the television on full blast so he can't sleep. What wretched
humanity! What a waste of energy that might have been dedicated
to a noble cause (eradicating illiteracy in the Congo, the battle
against smallpox in India, the taming of the indigenous Spanish clergy,
and so on)! (113-14)

The latest in this series is a trifling ballad, *Viaje a U. S. A.*
(*Trip to the U. S. A.*), 1967; the text and Goñi's drawings
provide the Spanish reader what he presumably expects: sky-
scrapers with shanties at their base, gangsters, Negro jazz sing-
ers, steatopygic women, and glowering black and white customs
officials. Seven hundred and sixteen lines of doggerel verse get
the author just through customs. He announces that he has in
preparation a work entitled *Nueva York amarga* (*Bitter New
York*).

In an interview at the Hispanic Society in New York, 1966,
Cela stated that he was working on a new novel with the intriguing title *La cesta de agua* (*The Basket of Water*), but
one year later he informed me that it had bogged down. He
is also translating into modern Spanish balladry the old epic
of the Cid, selections of which have already been published in
Papeles, and Tome I of his *Diccionario secreto* (*The Secret
Dictionary*), 1968, of commonly used obscene words is useful,
because the examples are drawn from popular and literary
sources. Such material will no doubt keep his name before the
public, a feat of sorts in a country flooded with so many works
that the offering of 175 literary prizes encourages. He has never
continued the memoirs, but firmly reiterates his intention to do so,
and is writing a war novel, *La octava de San Camilo* (*The
Octave of Saint Camilo*), precisely July 18, the day the Civil
War began in Spain and also his Saint's Day. It will be interesting to see how he treats the Civil War, because for all its

senselessness, war has its moments of heroism—a dimension not common in his works. A travel book on Barcelona similar to the one on Madrid is also in preparation.

Cela has reached a crisis in his literary career. Current output stems naturally, perhaps inevitably, from earlier inclinations. But his prose narratives, diverting though they may be, become more and more extravagant and even insubstantial. He formed a logical partnership between the pictorial representation of reality and his own portrayal of scenes of photographic, two-dimensional flatness, but he seems, at least for the time being, to have exhausted the possibilities of this genre. Cela's position in Spanish literary history is so secure that it is rather pointless for critics to insist that he write additional outstanding novels, but with his talent and vocation as a writer it would be remarkable if he did not.

Notes and References

Abbreviations

Clav	Clavileño
CHA	Cuadernos Hispanoamericanos
Hisp	Hispania
PPNCFL	Proceedings of the Pacific Northwest Conference on Foreign Languages
PSA	Papeles de Son Armadans
RHM	Revista Hispánica Moderna
WHR	Western Humanities Review

Chapter One

1. Something of the tentative nature of Cela's autobiographical sketches is to be seen even in the title "Relativo Curriculum Vitae," of the material supplied, with excellent photos, for the special number dedicated to him by *RHM*, XXVIII (1962), 179-209. In the *Obra completa* (Barcelona: Ediciones Destino, 1962), I, 531-41, the novelist reprints some of the earliest biographical sketches he wrote for his own works. More biographical information may be found in: *La cucaña, memorias de Camilo José Cela* (Barcelona: Ediciones Destino, 1959); M. Gómez-Santos, "Cela cuenta su vida," *Diálogos españoles* (Madrid: Ediciones Cid, 1958), pp. 121-71; Emilio Salcedo, *El "Viaje a Salamanca" de Camilo José Cela* (Salamanca: Centro de Estudios Salmantinos, 1957), 40 pp.; Annie Brierre, "A Madrid j'ai rencontré l'auteur du premier roman noir espagnol," *Nouvelles Littéraires* (le 29 janvier, 1959); Eduardo Trives, *Una semana con Camilo José Cela* (Alicante: Gráficos Vidal, 1960), 88 pp.; Ignacio Iglesias, "Diálogo con Camilo José Cela," *Cuadernos* (Paris), no. 43 (julio-agosto, 1960), 73-76; Jorge Mañach, *Visitas españolas* (Madrid: Revista de Occidente, 1960), pp. 328-42; Edouard Roditi, "Gespräch mit Camilo José Cela," *Du Schweitzerische Monatsschrift* (Zurich), XXI, no. 239 (Jan., 1961), 60-64; "Charla con Camilo José Cela y

Theodore S. Beardsley, Jr.," a recording of the Hispanic Society of America, New York, 1966. Cela has also been most helpful in supplying information in several personal interviews and correspondence since 1960.

2. This information is based on a revised chronology of his life that Cela sent me from Palma, Majorca, June 7, 1967. Note, however, that in *Obra completa*, I, 207, it is stated that the first stay in a sanitarium was at the age of fifteen, in 1931. Possibly a secretarial lapse is involved here.

3. *La cucaña*, pp. 153-55.

4. Cited by J. M. Castellet at the beginning of his discussion of tradition in Cela's travel books in "La obra narrativa de Camilo José Cela," *RHM*, XXVIII (1962), 107-50. Imitations of foreign works by Hispanic writers are bad because they result from a tendency to improvise on certain of the more striking aspects of the books imitated without first assimilating them to that which is peculiarly Spanish.

Chapter Two

1. See his Prologue to Paul Ilie's *Novelística de Camilo José Cela* (Madrid: Editorial Gredos, 1963), pp. 23-25. However, as Juan Goytisolo has pointed out in *Problemas de la novela* (Barcelona: Seix Barral, 1959), pp. 18-21, in the thirty years prior to *La colmena* novelists had been concerned only with a select minority of the middle or upper classes. The new writers rediscovered the way to portray the people as a whole.

2. Juan Luis Alborg, *Hora actual de la novela española* (Madrid: Taurus, 1958), p. 83, feels that Cela's influence on young writers is pernicious and that Cela will have a lot to answer for, but quotes the anecdote that in the first few years after its publication *La familia de Pascual Duarte* led to a thousand critical articles, but sold only three hundred copies. For F. C. Sáinz de Robles, *La novela española en el siglo XX* (Madrid: Pegaso, 1957), p. 240, the novel is too plebeian, violent, sensational. Gonzalo Torrente Ballester, *Panorama de la literatura española*, 2nd ed. (Madrid: Ediciones Guadarrama, 1961), I, 419-20, criticizes the realism of the book in the same terms, and adds that the material is as fantastic as *Peter Pan;* but he expresses a favorable reaction toward the prose style. These opinions are typical of those who saw the work as something potentially dangerous in the hands of subversive youth.

3. César Barja, *Libros y autores modernos* (Los Angeles: Camp-

bell's Bookstore, 1933), pp. 344-45. José A. Balseiro, *Novelistas espa-ñoles modernos* (New York: Macmillan Co., 1948), pp. 173-80.

4. Such also appear to be the implications when Pascual shoots his dog Chispa. Ilie, *La novelística*, p. 53.

5. Alborg, *Hora actual*, p. 84.

6. Ilie, *La novelística*, p. 38.

7. Robert Kirsner, *The Novels and Travels of Camilo José Cela* (Chapel Hill, N. C.: Univ. of North Carolina Press, 1963), p. 29.

8. Alborg, *Hora actual*, p. 85. Without some conditioning by Pascual's unfavorable environment, Alborg cannot explain the atroci-ties committed in the novel.

9. Alonso Zamora Vicente, *Camilo José Cela* (Madrid: Editorial Gredos, 1962), pp. 42-44. David M. Feldman, "Camilo José Cela and *La familia de Pascual Duarte*," *Hisp*, XLVI, no. 4 (1961), 656-59. The word "rematar" used by Pascual to refer to his killing of Don Jesús means to give the coup de grâce to a dying person or animal, but Pascual could still have been with a group of men who attacked the Count, although there is never any implication that others were involved.

10. Mary Ann Beck, "Nuevo encuentro con *La familia de Pascual Duarte*," *RHM*, XXX (1964), 288.

11. Prologue to *La familia de Pascual Duarte* (Buenos Aires: Espasa-Calpe, 1955), pp. 25-31.

12. Emilio González López, ed., *La familia de Pascual Duarte* (New York: Las Américas Publishing Co., 1965), pp. 129-30.

13. Mary Ann Beck, "Nuevo encuentro," p. 286.

14. *Ibid.*, p. 287.

15. Domingo Pérez Minik, *Novelistas españoles de los siglos XIX y XX* (Madrid: Ediciones Guadarrama, 1957), p. 264.

16. *La novelística*, pp. 234-35.

17. *Ibid.*, p. 42.

18. *Ibid.*, p. 40.

19. Eugenio G. de Nora, *La novela española contemporánea* (Ma-drid: Editorial Gredos, 1962), II, 114.

20. José Ortega, "Antecedentes y naturaleza del tremendismo en Cela," *Hisp*, XLVIII, no. 1 (1965), 21-28.

21. Olga P. Ferrer, "La literatura española tremendista y su nexo con el existencialismo," *RHM*, XXII (1956), 298.

22. Alfredo Rodríguez traces the theme of the child-eating hog from Galdós (*Obras completas* [Madrid, 1964], IV, 1246), through Valle-Inclán, Azorín, Lorca, Ayala, and Cela in "Esbozo de un tema mo-

derno: la antropofagia porcina," *Papers on Language and Literature,* II, no. 1 (1966), 269-73.

23. Jerónimo Mallo, "Caracterización y valor del 'tremendismo' en la novela española contemporánea," *Hisp,* XXXIX, no. 1 (1956), 53.

24. John Cruickshank, *Albert Camus and the Literature of Revolt* (London: Oxford University Press, 1959), pp. 6-7.

25. Louis R. Rossi, "La Peste de l'absurde," in *Configuration critique d'Albert Camus,* ed. J. H. Matthews (Paris: Lettres Modernes, 1961), I, 163. Published as nos. 64-66 of *La Revue des Lettres Modernes,* VIII (1961).

26. E. de Nora, in *La novela española,* II, 115, points out that Camus' novel was published only a few months before Cela's, which had already circulated for some time in search of a publisher. This statement is in reply to a critic who suggested plagiarism of Camus by Cela.

27. Cruickshank, *Albert Camus,* pp. 8-11.

28. Gerald E. Wade, "The Cult of Violence in the Contemporary Spanish Novel," *Tennessee Studies in Literature,* I (1956), 52.

29. Alborg, *Hora actual,* pp. 84-87, is one who has criticized most sharply lack of characterization in the novel.

30. Sister Mary Julia, in *"L'Etranger* y *La familia de Pascual Duarte:* un contraste de conceptos," *PSA,* XLIV, no. CXXXII (marzo, 1967), 265-304, has pointed out Pascual's fatalism and other similarities and differences between the works of Camus and Cela.

31. Julián Marías, *Filosofía actual y existencialismo en España* (Madrid: Revista de Occidente, 1955), pp. 22, 45.

32. Pérez Minik, *Novelistas españoles,* pp. 263-64.

Chapter Three

1. *The Novels,* p. 36.
2. Ilie, *La novelística,* pp. 83-88.
3. *La obra narrativa,* p. 146.

Chapter Four

1. Angel Valbuena Prat, in his Introduction to *La novela picaresca* (Madrid: Aguilar, 1962), pp. 14-15, reviews the social factors pointed out by nineteenth-century positivistic criticism.

2. Oldrich Belic, "Cervantes y la novela picaresca," *Philologica Pragensia,* VI, no. 2 (1963), 113-23.

3. José María de Cossío, "Prólogo" to Cela's *Nuevas andanzas y desventuras de Lazarillo de Tormes* (Madrid: Selecciones Airón, 1952), pp. 9-22. Cossío may represent, in part, a feeling by older generations that the picaresque genre gave Spain a bad press. Juan Goytisolo, *Problemas*, pp. 92-93, still feels that one can learn more about conditions in Spain of the sixteenth and seventeenth centuries by leafing through such novels than from any history book.

4. Américo Castro, "El Lazarillo de Tormes," *Semblanzas y estudios españoles* (Princeton: Ediciones Insula of Madrid, 1956), pp. 93-98.

5. Guillermo de Torre, "Vagabundeos críticos por el mundo de Cela," *RHM*, XXVIII (1962), 154-55.

6. Ilie, *La novelística*, p. 119.

7. Kirsner, *The Novels*, p. 54. Pablo Cabañas, "Camilo José Cela novelista," *CHA*, "Notas de lectura," II, no. 4 (1947), 113.

Chapter Five

1. Gómez-Santos, *Diálogos*, p. 134.

2. Zamora Vicente, *Camilo José Cela*, pp. 143-44.

3. When Kirsner, *The Novels*, p. 120, finds the "Apuntes" undeveloped compared to the *cuadros de costumbres* of the nineteenth century, something of the problem of equating Cela's sketches with the older works becomes evident.

4. I have the curious first edition which has the imprint on the title page, Madrid: Ricardo Aguilera, 1949, but on the spine the date 1951. Moñino's "Prólogo" is on pp. i-vii.

5. Gustavo Bueno Martínez attempts a systematic application of behaviorist principles to Cela's novel in "*La colmena*, novela behaviorista," *Clav*, III, no. 17 (1952), 53-58.

Chapter Six

1. Gonzalo Torrente Ballester, "*La colmena*, cuarta novela de Camilo José Cela," *CHA*, VIII, no. 22 (1951), 101. Alborg, *Hora actual*, p. 91, also suggests Huxley's *Point Counter Point*. John J. Flasher, in "Aspects of Novelistic Technique in Cela's *La colmena*," *Philological Papers*, XII (1959), 32-34, shows in detail that similarities with Dos Passos are largely fortuitous. Rodolfo Cardona, *Novelistas españoles de hoy* (New York: W. W. Norton, 1959), pp. 21-28, feels that Cela is superior to Dos Passos. He certainly is less rambling.

2. F. J. Solero, "*La colmena* de Camilo José Cela," *Sur*, no. 201 (julio, 1951), 112-13. Torrente Ballester, "*La colmena*, cuarta novela," pp. 96-97. Both writers feel that Cela has changed greatly since *La familia de Pascual Duarte*.

3. In the "Nota a la primera edición." I am using the Spanish edition (Barcelona-México: Editorial Noguer, 1955).

4. Nora, *La novela española*, II, 121.

5. Ferrer, "La literatura española tremendista," p. 300.

6. *The Hive*, translated by J. M. Cohen in consultation with Arturo Barea (New York: Farrar, Straus, and Young, 1953).

7. *La novelística*, p. 127.

8. John S. Brushwood and José Rojas Garcidueñas, *Breve historia de la novela mexicana* (México: Ediciones de Andrea, 1959), p. 140.

9. J. van Praag Chantraine, "El pícaro en la novela española moderna," *RHM*, XXIX (1963), 26.

10. Kirsner, *The Novels*, p. 67.

11. *Mrs. Caldwell habla con su hijo* (Barcelona: Ediciones Destino, 1958), p. 14.

12. Alborg, *Hora actual*, p. 92. Sáinz de Robles, *La novela española*, pp. 239-40.

13. Alborg, *ibid*. See note 1 above.

14. Flasher, "Aspects," p. 36, thinks Martín turns optimist when he visits his mother's grave, but José Ortega, in "Importancia del personaje de Martín Marco en *La colmena* de Cela," *Romance Notes*, VI (1965), 92-95, shows that at the end he is still following the "Uncertain Roads" of the book's subtitle.

15. Ilie, *La novelística*, p. 139.

16. Marius Chatignon, "Camilo José Cela: *La Ruche*," *L'Esprit* (février, 1959), 380-81.

17. José Ortega, "*La colmena* de Camilo José Cela: contenido y expresión," unpublished Ph.D. dissertation, Ohio State University, 1963, p. 53.

18. Kirsner, *The Novels*, p. 66.

19. Hugh Thomas, *The Spanish Civil War* (London: Eyre and Spottiswood, 1961), pp. 632-33.

20. Ilie, *La novelística*, p. 143.

21. Gómez Santos, *Diálogos*, p. 143.

Chapter Seven

1. References are to the second edition (Barcelona: Ediciones Destino, 1958).

2. Alborg, *Hora actual,* pp. 95-96. Nora, *La novela española,* II, 124-26. Marcelo Arroita-Jáuregui, in "Los libros de la quincena," *Correo Literario,* IV, no. 78 (15 de agosto, 1953), 4, thought that it was perhaps the most profound psychological novel Cela had written up to that time.

3. Ilie, *La novelística,* pp. 150-208.

4. Castellet, *La obra narrativa,* pp. 144-46.

5. Ilie, *La novelística,* pp. 159-60.

6. *Ibid.,* pp. 166-67.

7. *Ibid.,* p. 169.

8. *Ibid.,* pp. 174-75.

9. *Ibid.,* p. 180.

10. *Ibid.,* pp. 174-75.

11. Kirsner, *The Novels,* p. 86.

12. *Ibid.*

13. *Ibid.*

14. *Libros de poesía* (Madrid: Aguilar, 1959), pp. 1148-49.

15. Ilie, *La novelística,* pp. 189-92.

Chapter Eight

1. Gómez Santos, *Diálogos,* p. 154.

2. José Luis Cano, in *Insula,* no. 113 (15 de mayo, 1955), 6-7, and Germán Bleiberg, in *Clav,* VI, no. 36 (nov.-dic., 1955), 77, evidently impressed by the scope of the book, felt that it was Cela's best to date. Perhaps they believed, too, that it was a welcome change after the style of "Nadalismo" characterized by "studied addiction to plotlessness and inertia," which had become typical of the novels awarded the Nadal Prize, according to Mariano García, "The Modern Novel," *Atlantic Monthly,* 207, no. 1 (Jan., 1961), 121-24. Other critics somehow feel that Cela has achieved a significant stylistic and linguistic creation whether authentic or not: José María Martínez Cachero, in *Archivum* (Oviedo), V (1955), 202-4; C. Otero, *CHA,* XXV, no. 72 (1955), 351-56; Alonso Zamora Vicente, *Insula,* no. 115 (15 de julio, 1955), 3. J.-L. Vázquez-Dodero, in *Table Ronde* (janvier, 1960), 72-78, dislikes *Pascual Duarte,* but includes a translation in French of a passage from the beginning of *La Catira.* Other critics attack the "artificial" language, feel that the author has misunderstood Venezuela and its people, has not provided authentic characters, and has attempted to imitate *Doña Bárbara* of Rómulo Gallegos: Fernando Baeza, *Indice de Artes y Letras,* X, no. 82 (sept.,

1955), 27; Sebastián Cienfuegos, "Le Roman en Espagne," *Europe*, XXXVI, nos. 345-346 (jan.-fév., 1958), 17-29; F. Delgado, *Estudios Americanos*, X, no. 48 (1955), 311-20; Guillermo Morón, *Indice de Artes y Letras*, X, no. 81 (julio, 1955), 21; José Antonio Pérez Regalado, *Doña Bárbara y La Catira, dos novelas sobre el llano de Venezuela* (Caracas: Ediciones Orinoco, 1960), 99 pp. Pérez Regalado, however, has not indicated more than a casual resemblance between *Doña Bárbara* and Cela's novel.

3. The edition cited is that of Barcelona: Editorial Noguer, 1955.

4. Olga Prjevalinsky Ferrer, *El sistema estético de Camilo José Cela* (Valencia: Editorial Castalia, 1960).

5. Prologue to *Mrs. Caldwell*, pp. 11-12.

6. *Mis páginas preferidas* (Madrid: Editorial Gredos, 1956), p. 179.

7. Arturo Torres-Ríoseco, "Camilo José Cela, primer novelista español contemporáneo," *RHM*, XXVIII (1962), 169. Pérez Regalado points out that La Catira speaks on occasion an inappropriate brothel language, *Doña Bárbara*, p. 75.

8. Ilie, *La novelística*, p. 161.

Chapter Nine

1. Luis Felipe Vivanco, "Una tierra, un escritor, un libro, una edición," *CHA*, nos. 128-129 (ag.-sept., 1960), 156. See also Pedro Laín Entralgo, "Carta de un pedantón a un vagabundo por tierras de España," *Ejercicios de comprensión* (Madrid: Taurus, 1959), pp. 151-70.

2. From the school edition of *Viaje a la Alcarria* by Philip Polack (Boston: D. C. Heath, 1962), pp. 14-15. For more details, consult the Introduction of Paul Ilie to Frances M. López-Morillas' translation, *Journey to the Alcarria* (Madison: University of Wisconsin Press, 1964), pp. vii-xix.

3. "A Bus Trip," translated by Anthony Kerrigan in the special number on Spain of *The Texas Quarterly*, IV (1961), 166.

4. Kirsner, *The Novels*, p. 129.

5. *Páginas de geografía errabunda* (Madrid-Barcelona: Ediciones Alfaguara, 1965), p. 60.

6. *Viaje al Pirineo de Lérida* (Madrid: Ediciones Alfaguara, 1965), p. 205.

7. From an interview of Isabel Magaña Schevill, "Cela y los *Papeles de Son Armadans*," *Hisp*, XLI, no. 3 (1958), 317.

8. *Obra completa* (Barcelona: Ediciones Destino, 1965), IV, 521-

30. Cela speaks in some detail of other convents or churches which have been shipped off, particularly to the United States.

9. Kirsner, *The Novels*, p. 167, implies rather vaguely that Cela becomes a standard-bearer of Castro's concept of history.

10. *Ibid.*, pp. 170-71.

11. (Barcelona-Mexico: Noguer, 1959), p. 22.

12. *Páginas de geografía errabunda*, pp. 243-314.

13. See note 6 above.

Chapter Ten

1. Claudio Guillén, "Luis Sánchez, Ginés de Pasamonte y los inventores del género picaresco," *Homenaje a Rodríguez-Moñino* (Valencia: Artes Gráficas Soler, 1966), I, 223-24, cites cases of Goya and Giotto without successors, in the case of the latter for as much as a century.

2. (Barcelona-Madrid-México: Editorial Noguer, 1964).

3. In a recorded interview with Theodore S. Beardsley, Jr., of the Hispanic Society of America in New York, 1966. The recording may be purchased from the Society.

4. Antonio Fernández Molina, "En su tobogán," *PSA*, XXIX, no. LXXXVI (1963), 205.

5. *La cucaña*, pp. 18-19.

6. Fernández Molina, "En su tobogán," p. 199.

7. (Barcelona-México: Editorial Noguer, 1960, 1961), Series I and II.

8. David W. Foster, "Cela's Changing Concept of the Novel," *Hisp*, XLIX, no. 2 (1966), 244-49.

9. Carmen Iglesias has summarized earlier definitions and further developed the concept of the *esperpento* in her excellent article, "El 'esperpento' en la obra de Valle-Inclán," *Cuadernos Americanos*, no. 4 (1959), 1-39. See also these recent lengthy studies: Guillermo Díaz Plaja, *Las estéticas de Valle-Inclán* (Madrid: Editorial Gredos, 1965), pp. 78-91, 131-39, 147-51, 228-41; Antonio Risco, *La estética de Valle-Inclán en los esperpentos y en "El ruedo ibérico"* (Madrid: Editorial Gredos, 1966), pp. 25-127, 225-76; Emilio González López, *El arte dramático de Valle-Inclán* (New York: Las Américas Publishing Co., 1967), pp. 147-267.

10. Antonio Amado, "Camilo José Cela, académico," *CHA*, XXXI, no. 88 (1957), 83.

11. Mariano Baquero Goyanes, "La novela española de 1939 a 1953," *CHA*, no. 67 (1955), 89.

12. (Madrid-Barcelona: Ediciones Alfaguara, 1965, 1966), Series I, II; III, IV, V, VI, VII.

13. Stuart Gilbert, *James Joyce's "Ulysses"* (New York: A. Knopf, 1952), pp. 44-51.

14. Michel Butor, *Répertoire* (Paris: Editions de Minuit, 1960), p. 206.

Selected Bibliography

Primary Sources

The Writings of Camilo José Cela

Only the most important works are listed by first edition. The numerous pieces which appeared in newspapers and periodicals are now being collected in the *Obra completa*. Available English translations are also indicated. A more complete list of the books published in 1962 and earlier may be found in Fernando Huarte Morton's "Bibliografía," *RHM*, XXVIII (1962), 210-20. Subtitles, some quite long, are omitted. Where pertinent, they are given in the text.

1. Collections

Mis páginas preferidas (Madrid: Editorial Gredos, 1956). Selections from the novels, travel books, short stories, and a few essays. Particularly interesting are the additional prologues for each.

Obra completa (Barcelona: Ediciones Destino, 1962, 1964, 1965, 1966, 1968), Vols. I; II; III, IV; V; VI. In the text this series is cited by volume and page number. This collection, still in process of publication, contains the first three novels, the short stories, the sketches of "apuntes carpetovetónicos," short novels, the travel books, *Avila*, and *Cuaderno del Guadarrama* (*Guadarrama Notebook*). Cela particularly recommends the collected works and has provided footnotes indicating textual corrections. There is also a complete list of editions and translations, and prologues are reprinted to which new ones are added.

2. Books

Avila (Barcelona: Editorial Noguer, 1952). English translation by John Forrester, same publisher and date.

Baraja de invenciones (*A Pack of Tales*), Valencia: Editorial Castalia, 1953.

El bonito crimen del carabinero (Barcelona: José Janés, 1947).

Café de artistas (Madrid: Editorial Tecnos, 1953).

Cajón de sastre (Grab Bag), Madrid: Ediciones Cid, 1957.

La Catira (Barcelona: Editorial Noguer, 1955).

El ciudadano Iscariote Reclús (Madrid: Ediciones Alfaguara, 1965).

La colmena (Buenos Aires: Emecé, 1951). English translation by J. M. Cohen with an introduction by Arturo Barea (New York: Farrar, Straus, and Young, 1953). There is a Spanish edition, with footnotes in English and vocabulary by José Ortega (New York: Las Américas Publishing Co., 1965).

Las compañías convenientes (Barcelona: Ediciones Destino, 1963).

Cuatro figuras del '98 (Barcelona: Editorial Aedos, 1961).

La cucaña—memorias (Barcelona: Ediciones Destino, 1959).

Del Miño al Bidasoa (Barcelona: Editorial Noguer, 1952).

Diccionario secreto (Madrid: Ediciones Alfaguara, 1968), tomo I.

Esas nubes que pasan (Madrid: Afrodisio Aguado, 1945).

La familia de Pascual Duarte (Madrid-Burgos: Editorial Aldecoa, 1942). Bilingual edition (New York: Las Américas Publishing Co., 1965). There is a new English translation by Anthony Kerrigan (Boston: Little, Brown, 1964). Also (New York: Avon Books, 1966). For student use there is the edition with vocabulary and notes by Harold L. Boudreau and John W. Kronik (New York: Appleton-Century-Crofts, 1961).

La familia del héroe (The Hero's Family), Madrid: Ediciones Alfaguara, 1965.

El gallego y su cuadrilla (Madrid: Ricardo Aguilera, 1949). On the spine is the date 1951, the year the book was actually published.

Garito de hospicianos (Barcelona: Editorial Noguer, 1963).

Gavilla de fábulas sin amor (Palma de Mallorca: Papeles de Son Armadans, 1962).

Historias de España Los ciegos, Los tontos (Madrid: Ediciones Arión, 1958).

Izas, rabizas y colipoterras (Barcelona: Editorial Lumen, 1964).

Judíos, moros y cristianos (Barcelona: Ediciones Destino, 1956).

Madrid (Madrid: Ediciones Alfaguara, 1966).

Mesa revuelta (Madrid: Ediciones de los estudiantes españoles, 1945).

El molino de viento (The Windmill), Barcelona: Editorial Noguer, 1956.

Mrs. Caldwell habla con su hijo (Barcelona: Ediciones Destino, 1953).

Nuevas andanzas y desventuras de Lazarillo de Tormes (Madrid: Ediciones La Nave, 1944).

Nuevas escenas matritenses (Madrid: Ediciones Alfaguara, 1965, 1966). Series I-II; III-VII.

Nuevo retablo de don Cristobita (Barcelona: Ediciones Destino, 1957). Contains earlier collections, *Esas nubes que pasan, El bonito crimen del carabinero, Baraja de invenciones.*

Once cuentos de fútbol (Madrid: Editora Nacional, 1963).

Pabellón de reposo (Madrid: Afrodisio Aguado, 1943). Not for public sale. In March of 1944 another edition was issued by the same publisher. Available in a bilingual edition entitled *Rest Home* (New York: Las Américas Publishing Co., 1961).

Páginas de geografía errabunda (Madrid: Ediciones Alfaguara, 1965).

Pisando la dudosa luz del día (Barcelona: Ediciones del Zodíaco, 1945). Most of the poems of this volume were written by 1936.

Primer viaje andaluz (Barcelona: Editorial Noguer, 1959).

La rueda de los ocios (Barcelona: Editorial Mateu, 1957).

Santa Balbina 37, gas en cada piso (*Santa Balbina 37, Gas in Every Flat*), Melilla: Mirto y Laurel, 1952.

El solitario (Palma de Mallorca: Papeles de Son Armadans, 1963).

Timoteo el incomprendido (Madrid: Editorial Rollán, 1952).

Tobogán de hambrientos (Barcelona: Editorial Noguer, 1962).

Toreo de salón (Barcelona: Editorial Lumen, 1963).

Viaje a la Alcarria (Madrid: Revista de Occidente, 1948). English translation by Frances M. López-Morillas (Madison: The University of Wisconsin Press, 1964). Available in a school edition with vocabulary and notes by Philip Polack (Boston: D. C. Heath Co., 1962).

Viaje a U. S. A. (Madrid: Ediciones Alfaguara, 1967).

Viaje al Pirineo de Lérida (Madrid: Ediciones Alfaguara, 1965).

Los viejos amigos (Barcelona: Editorial Noguer, 1960, 1961). Series I, II.

Secondary Sources

Listed here, for the most part, are books and articles not in the bibliography of *Revista Hispánica Moderna* of 1962. Many of those cited in the "Notes and References" are not repeated. Short reviews are omitted unless of particular interest. For additional titles readers are referred to the bibliographies in the *Publications of the Modern Language Association* and *The Year's Work in Romance Languages and Literatures.*

1. Books

FOSTER, DAVID W. *Forms of the Novel in the Work of Camilo José Cela* (Columbia, Mo.: University of Missouri Press, 1967). Excellent, perceptive observations and much suggestive criticism, but there is little in Cela's many statements about the novel to indicate the particular awareness of the Jungian collective unconscious and archetypes or Brechtian alienation of Foster's basic thesis.

ILIE, PAUL. *La novelística de Camilo José Cela* (Madrid: Editorial Gredos, 1963). The most penetrating book to date on Cela. Some may not agree with the author's interpretation of ontological and primitivistic aspects. The travel books are not discussed.

KIRSNER, ROBERT. *The Novels of Camilo José Cela* (Chapel Hill: The University of North Carolina Press, 1963). Very personal interpretations and reactions which readers may feel should be qualified at the very least.

PRJEVALINSKY FERRER, OLGA. *El sistema estético de Camilo José Cela* (Valencia: Editorial Castalia, 1960). One may not agree with her enthusiasm for *La Catira*, but it is not a bad choice for a stylistic study. The authoress presents a detailed analysis of linguistic and syntactical structure that is useful for reference.

ZAMORA VICENTE, ALONSO. *Camilo José Cela (acercamiento a un escritor)* (Madrid: Editorial Gredos, 1962). A broad commentary on Cela's works by an unqualified admirer. Balanced criticism is almost completely lacking.

2. Articles

AMADO, A. "Camilo José Cela, académico," *CHA*, XXXI, no. 88 (1957), 83-85. Humorous impressions about reactions to Cela's reception into the Academy.

BECK, MARY ANN. "Nuevo encuentro con *La familia de Pascual Duarte*," *RHM*, XXX (1964), 279-98. An interesting study of irony in this novel, but it gets a bit out of hand.

BERNSTEIN, J. S. "The Matricide of Pascual Duarte," *Homenaje a Rodríguez-Moñino* (Madrid: Editorial Castalia, 1966), I, 75-82. Even a rereading does not reveal the author's precise point. Apparently Pascual has latent incestuous attraction toward his sister and mother. He is an Orestean hero.

——. "Pascual Duarte and Orestes," *Symposium*, XXII (1968), 301-18. A serious attempt to mythicize Pascual. More pertinent here are the suggestions about Pascual's killing of Don Jesús.

CIRRE, JOSE FRANCISCO. "El protagonista múltiple en la reciente novela española," *PSA*, XXXIII, no. XCVIII (1964), 159-70. Discusses four contemporary Spanish novels, beginning with *La colmena*. Implications of the multiple protagonist could be further developed.

DELGADO, F. "*La Catira* de Camilo José Cela," *Estudios Americanos* (Sevilla), X, no. 48 (1955), 311-20. A reasoned, unfavorable criticism of this novel.

DONAHUE, FRANCIS. "Cela and Spanish 'Tremendismo'," *WHR*, XX, no. 4 (1966), 301-6. Mostly a survey of *Pascual Duarte* with very little on "tremendismo."

FERNANDEZ MOLINA, ANTONIO. "En su tobogán," *PSA*, XXIX, no. LXXXVI (1963), 191-206. An enthusiastic, rather uncritical review of Cela's novel.

FLIGHTNER, JAMES A. "The Travel Books of Camilo José Cela," *PPNCFL*, XVII (1966), 187-92. This article and others indicate that a lengthy study should be devoted to the travel books.

FOSTER, DAVID WILLIAM. "Cela's Changing Concept of the Novel," *Hisp*, XLIX, no. 2 (1966), 244-49. Has difficulty in determining, from a study of *Garito de hospicianos* (1963), Cela's latest novelistic tendencies. A number of articles by the same critic based on his dissertation are in the process of publication.

————. Review of Camilo José Cela, *La familia del héroe*, *Books Abroad*, XL, no. 3 (1966), 318-19. Summarizes well Cela's relative lack of development in the last five years.

GONZALEZ LOPEZ, EMILIO. "Camilo José Cela," in his edition of *La familia de Pascual Duarte* (New York: Las Américas Publishing Co., 1965), pp. 123-44. Rather repetitious and hasty.

HOYOS, ANTONIO DE. "*Cintas Rojas, Pascual Duarte* y el campesino de Cagitán," *Correo Literario*, V, no. 76 (15 de julio, 1953), 1. One of the first to compare the killer in López Pinilla's novel with Pascual Duarte. Also cites a historical mass murderer.

ILIE, PAUL. "Introduction" to *Journey to the Alcarria*, translated by Frances M. López-Morillas (Madison: University of Wisconsin Press, 1964), pp. vii-xix. A good over-all presentation of the region and Cela's themes, but necessarily perfunctory in dealing with other works.

KIRSNER, ROBERT. "*La Catira*, novela américo-hispana," *PSA*, XXXVIII, no. CXII (1965), 87-93. A defense of *La Catira* on the grounds that, disillusioned with the limited and uncomprehending public in Spain, Cela came to Venezuela in search of a wider audience, "to create an epic Venezuelan novel."

Kirsner stresses that Cela had two publics in mind. It is for precisely this reason, one can add, that the novel falls between two chairs.

Laín Entralgo, Pedro. "Carta de un pedantón a un vagabundo por tierras de España," *Ejercicios de comprensión* (Madrid: Ediciones Taurus, 1959), pp. 151-70. Praises Cela for his love of underdeveloped rural areas. Lack of love is Spain's greatest problem.

Nora, Eugenio G. de. "Camilo José Cela," in *La novela española contemporánea, 1927-1960* (Madrid: Gredos, 1962), II, 111-30. One of the better-rounded discussions in recent manuals of Cela's works.

Ortega, Jose. "Antecedentes y naturaleza del tremendismo en Cela," *Hisp*, XLVIII, no. 1 (1965), 21-28. A useful survey of passages in Spanish literature of all periods with "tremendista" affinities, but might point out more how Cela differs from them.

————. "Importancia del personaje Martín Marco en *La colmena* de Cela," *Romance Notes*, VI (1965), 92-95. Shows clearly that Martín is and will remain a character without purpose in life.

————. "El sentido temporal en *La colmena*," *Symposium*, XIX (1965), 115-22. Analyzes with insight a variety of technical devices used to link the characters and time in the novel.

Otero, C. "*La Catira*, novela de Camilo José Cela," *CHA*, XXV, no. 72 (1955), 351-56. Enthusiasm for this novel, but his remarks imply their own contradiction.

Praag Chantraine, J. van. "El pícaro en la novela española moderna," *RHM*, XXIX (1963), 23-31. Inaccurate details and not very perceptive about Cela's works.

Predmore, R. L. "La imagen del hombre en las obras de Camilo José Cela," *La Torre*, IX, no. 33 (1961), 81-102. This study shows that Cela's view of man is extremely pessimistic. One notes that by choosing citations of a certain kind it is possible to give an unbalanced portrayal of a writer.

Trives, Eduardo. *Una semana con Camilo José Cela* (Alicante: Gráficos Vidal, 1960), 88 pp. A pleasant, impressionistic account of a week with Cela, but without solid information.

Urbistondo, Vicente. "Cela y Rubens: estudio analítico sobre *Tobogán de hambrientos*," *PSA*, XXXIX, no. CXVII (1965), 252-77. The title is misleading. There is very little about Rubens in the article, and the connection with him is purely arbitrary.

Uribe Echevarria, Juan. "Cela y su Madrid en tercer grado (*La colmena*)," *Atenea* (Concepción, Chile), año XXVIII, CII, nos.

313-314 (julio-agosto, 1951), 103-9. Exaggerates influence of Baroja and Cela's pitiless account of people in Madrid.

WOODCOCK, GEORGE. "The Nihilism of Modern Spain," *New Republic*, (July 12, 1954), 16-17. Stresses great change in Spanish life, particularly urban, after the Civil War, of which *The Hive* is an expression.

Index